Burntisland
Port of Grace

The Story of the Royal Burgh of Burntisland to the Union of Parliaments in 1707

Based on James Speed's Notes on the History of Burntisland, Transcribed by Alexander Foster in 1869

Iain Sommerville

with Ian Archibald and Helen Mabon

Published by Burntisland Heritage Trust

with financial assistance from Burntisland Development Trust, Fife Council, ExxonMobil and Shell

Published in 2004 by Burntisland Heritage Trust
4 Kirkgate, Burntisland, Fife, KY3 9DB, Scotland

British Library Cataloguing in Publication Data:
A catalogue record of this book is available from the British Library.

ISBN 0-9539353-1-0

Designed by Iain Sommerville and Ian Archibald.
Printed in Scotland by Thos McGilvray & Son Ltd, Wemyss Road, Dysart, Fife, KY1 2XZ.

Iain Sommerville, BA (Hons), DMS, is a Trustee of Burntisland Heritage Trust. He was brought up in Carradale, Argyll, and is a graduate of Stirling University. He is now retired after a career in the Scottish Office in Glasgow and Edinburgh. Iain's mother was born at 7 Grange Road, Burntisland, and he is the fourth generation of his family to make their home in the town. His interest in Burntisland's history began when researching the story of his grandfather, James Lothian Mitchell, who was a controversial figure in the political and educational life of Burntisland in the late 19th and early 20th centuries.

Ian Archibald is a founder member and the Convener of Burntisland Heritage Trust. He was educated at Kirkcaldy High School and pursued a nomadic and lifelong career in land surveying and cartography. He eventually settled in Burntisland with his wife Dorothy in 1987, and is now retired. He has been unable to prove conclusively that David Archibald, who was accused of stealing stones from the Burntisland breakwater for use as ship's ballast in 1601, is not a distant cousin! More seriously, his greatest ambition - to locate the wreck of Charles I's ferry, the 'Blessing' - is yet to be realised.

Helen Mabon (née Forsyth) is the Secretary of Burntisland Heritage Trust. She is the third generation of her family to be born and bred in Burntisland, and her early years were spent at Glassliehead Farm. She attended Burntisland Primary School and Kirkcaldy High School, and then worked at the local National Commercial Bank. She married Peter Mabon and is now in partnership with him as Mabon Consultants, a Burntisland based provider of training courses. Her lifelong interest in history finds practical expression in her work for Burntisland Heritage Trust.

Burntisland Heritage Trust was established in 1993 as an informal group, and assumed formal trust status in 1998. It is a registered charity (Scottish Charity reference SC 028539), and is run by committed volunteers. It aims to protect and promote all aspects of Burntisland's heritage.

Cover illustrations

Front: 'Burntisland Tolbooth' by Andrew Young. Burntisland Heritage Trust Collection.
Front inside: 'Burnt Island' by John Slezer. National Galleries of Scotland.
Back: detail from 'View of Burntisland' by Andrew Wilson. National Galleries of Scotland.
Back inside: 'Burnt Island, Enchkieth' by John Slezer. National Galleries of Scotland.

Contents

James Speed

James Speed was born in Edinburgh in 1787, the son of George Speed and Agnes Anderson. The family moved to the parish of Dalgety in Fife, where James' sister, Helen Thrift Speed, was born in 1793. James became a merchant in Burntisland. In due course he was elected to the town council. He also gained a reputation as a respected local historian, and on behalf of the town council he was responsible for giving evidence on historical matters to the Royal Commission on Municipal Corporations in Scotland, which reported in 1835.

He served as Provost of Burntisland from 1837 to 1840. In 1862, his home was in the High Street and he was described as a person of independent means. James and Helen Speed had their own seat in the Parish Church.

James died on 1 December 1867 at the age of 80, and is buried in Burntisland Parish Churchyard in East Leven Street. He appears to have been unmarried. His sister Helen died just three weeks after her brother, and is interred beside him. She was also unmarried, and probably kept house fo James.

Their impressive headstone (pictured above) was erected in 1870 by Mary Tullidilph Watson of Halbeath.

Preface

Burntisland is a small resort town in Fife, Scotland. It is situated on the north side of the Forth estuary, opposite Edinburgh. Its population at the time of writing in 2004 is about 6,000. Over the years, its strategic maritime location has given it an importance in national affairs much greater than one would expect, and has contributed significantly to the town's rich and colourful heritage.

Twentieth century writers on the history of the town often made reference to "Speed's notes" as one of their sources, but no-one in the town could recall ever seeing them. The reorganisation of local government in 1975 had led to the dispersal, and in some cases destruction, of many of the Burntisland Burgh records. It was only on the establishment of the Fife Council Archive Centre and the appointment of an archivist in October 2000 that the old records in the custody of the Council were brought together in one location, and properly listed and indexed.

Among those records was a leather-bound foolscap volume entitled "Documents relating to the history of Burntisland, Transcribed by Alexander Foster 1869". It contained "Notes relating to the Royal Burgh of Burntisland chiefly compiled from the Burgh Records by James Speed". This ran to 235 pages in Foster's fine copperplate handwriting. As Speed died in 1867, and the volume is dated 1869, it is clear that Foster decided to create a permanent record from notes left by Speed.

Burntisland Heritage Trust took the view that the contents were of considerable value, and represented the first written history of Burntisland. As it had never before been published, the Trustees decided to remedy that. This book is the result.

Speed's notes give us a brief history of Burntisland's early years, followed by a detailed diary of the town from the late 16th century to the early 18th century. They provide a fascinating tale of the trials and tribulations of local folk in a small Scottish burgh in that period - a period which is one of the most exciting in Burntisland's long and colourful history.

Although we were keen to bring Speed's notes before a wider audience, they were not in a form which would immediately appeal to readers in the 21st century. We therefore decided to prepare a concise and richly illustrated text, drawing mainly on Speed's notes but also on other sources, which would cover the period of the notes in an easily read form. That illustrated text constitutes the main part of this book.

Of necessity, most of the illustrations are from a later period or are artists' impressions - but they have been carefully selected or commissioned to convey something of the flavour of the town in earlier years.

So that the reader can also explore Speed's original notes, we have included them in their entirety as an appendix. They provide us with a history of the town - mainly in the 17th century - which was written by an educated and articulate man who was much closer to the events which he recorded than we are.

Finally, a special word of thanks from me to my fellow Trustees, Ian Archibald and Helen Mabon, for their contributions to the realisation of this project. The fact that we were able to complete it within six months of getting confirmation of funding was due in no small measure to their efforts.

Iain Sommerville
Trustee, Burntisland Heritage Trust

Burntisland, October 2004

Acknowledgements

Many people assisted us with this project. We record our sincere thanks to them all.

James Speed's notes on the history of Burntisland are reproduced by kind permission of Fife Council. The Fife Council archivist, Andrew Dowsey, and his colleague, Lisa Wood, played an important part in the realisation of the project, and provided much advice and assistance.

There would have been no book without the generous financial support of Burntisland Development Trust (on behalf of Alcan Inc), Fife Council, ExxonMobil Chemical Ltd and Shell U.K. Ltd.

The talents of our illustrators compensated handsomely for the absence of pictures from the 16th, 17th and 18th centuries. They were Keli Clark of Burntisland, Douglas Gray of Kinghorn, and Ian McLeod of Burntisland.

We are also very grateful to the following for permission to reproduce their earlier works - Ian McLeod of Burntisland, Gavin Anderson of Milnathort, Lindsay Brydon of Edinburgh, and Eric Bell of Cluny. The works of Anna Crawford Briggs of Burntisland are reproduced by kind permission of MacKenzie McGill Galleries.

Frank Baird of Aberdeen spent many hours working on the designs of the front and back covers, suggested improvements to the text, and gave good-humoured support throughout the term of the project.

Dr David Caldwell of the National Museums of Scotland provided significant assistance, advice and encouragement.

Thomas Dunbar of Burntisland helped with the illustrations. Fraser Gold of Milngavie and Professor Christina Sommerville of Alva read drafts of the text, and made many helpful suggestions.

Douglas Speirs and Steve Liscoe of the Fife Council Archaeology Unit ensured that our references to the early times were accurate, and made photographs available to us. Robin Blair, Lord Lyon King of Arms, supplied valuable information on arms and seals.

Alan Barker and Edward Wilson, both of Burntisland, allowed us to use items from their collections. Bill Kirkhope of Dalgety Bay supplied one of the photographs. The late Cathy Watson of Burntisland gave us permission some years ago to use material from her collection, and a copy of one of her pictures appears in the book.

We acknowledge the help and co-operation of the staff of the following organisations who kindly permitted us to provide illustrations based on items in their collections - Kirkcaldy Museum & Art Gallery, the National Archives of Scotland, the National Galleries of Scotland, the Trustees of the National Library of Scotland, the National Museums of Scotland, the Stenhouse Conservation Centre, the Royal Commission on the Ancient and Historical Monuments of Scotland, and the British Library.

The source of each illustration is recorded with its caption.

George Milne and Teresa Henderson of our printers, Thos McGilvray & Son Ltd, gave us helpful advice on many occasions.

Finally, we acknowledge our debt to earlier writers on the history of Burntisland, in particular Andrew Young, John Blyth and Robert Livingstone. Their works are listed in the Bibliography.

Notes for the Reader

The main problem we faced in producing this book was how to present a 19th century manuscript in a manner which would have general appeal today. We therefore decided to make the main part of the book a specially written text containing selected extracts from the original manuscript, and we hope we have succeeded in blending these into a comprehensive and readable whole. We have also added a large number of illustrations which are intended to give a flavour of the period (although many of them are, of necessity, from later years). A Timeline has been included so that the reader can place local events in the national context.

The complete text of the original manuscript is included as Appendix A.

The book covers the period to the Union of Parliaments in 1707. With a few topics, where we thought it would be helpful to the reader, we have followed developments through to later years.

We hope that the following notes will be useful to you, the reader, in understanding some of the methods which we have used to make the book easy to read.

Shaded boxes   The shaded boxes in Chapters I to VIII contain edited extracts from James Speed's original manuscript. The square brackets in these boxes have been used to enclose clarifying additions which we have made to the original text.

Glossary   The book contains unfamiliar words and phrases, and also more common words and phrases used in unfamiliar ways. To avoid overloading the text with explanatory footnotes, we have prepared a comprehensive glossary at Appendix B. There is an explanation of the various currencies referred to in the book at Appendix C.

Footnotes   These are mainly used to explain apparent contradictions, and to provide corrections in cases where Speed's original text contained known errors.

Text omitted   "....." indicates that part of the original text has been omitted.

Dates   "c" (for circa) before a date indicates that the date is approximate.

References to other authors   In the main text there are references to other authors, and in particular to Andrew Young, John Blyth and Robert Livingstone. In all such cases, full details of their works are contained in the Bibliography.

Bibliography   The Bibliography also contains details of works which are recommended for further reading.

Illustrations   The source of each illustration is given with its caption. The sources are also acknowledged on page 6.

Timeline to 1707

Scotland/Britain   ## Burntisland

↓   ↓

Skara Brae settlement constructed –	**c3200 BC**	
Stonehenge erected –	**c3100 BC**	
Start of the Bronze Age –	**c2500 BC**	
	c2000 BC –	Bronze Age inhabitants left carvings and cremation remains
Start of the Iron Age –	**c750 BC**	
	c450 BC –	Early Iron Age inhabitants built a fort on Dunearn Hill

Birth of Jesus Christ

Romans invaded England –	**43**	
	83 –	Roman visit
Battle of Mons Graupius –	**84**	
Construction of Hadrian's Wall –	**122**	
St Columba left Ireland for Scotland –	**563**	
Death of St Adamnan –	**704**	
Union of Scots and Picts –	**843**	
David I became King –	**1124**	
	1130 –	King David I granted the lands of Kinghorn Wester to Dunfermline Abbey
	1243 –	Kirkton Church consecrated and dedicated to St Adamnan
Alexander III became King –	**1249**	
	c1250 –	Rossend Castle built
	1286 –	Alexander III killed at Pettycur
Auld Alliance (Scotland/France) –	**1295**	
Battle of Bannockburn –	**1314**	

	1382	– Rossend Castle enlarged
	1506	– Burgh of Regality
'Great Michael' launched at Newhaven –	1511	
James V became King –	1513	
	1541	– First Royal Burgh Charter
Mary became Queen of Scots –	1542	
	c1550	– Rossend Castle rebuilt
Reformation –	1560	
	1562	– Chastellard executed
Witches punishable by execution –	1563	
James VI became King –	1567	
	1573	– Burgh of Regality
	1585	– Second Royal Burgh Charter
	1586	– Formation of first Town Council of the Royal Burgh; John Clapen elected Provost
	1589	– Ferry disaster
	1592	– New Parish Church begun
	1597	– One witch burned
	1598	– Fabric of new Parish Church completed; one witch burned alive
	1601	– The Church's General Assembly met in Burntisland; James VI proposed a new translation of the Bible

1603 Union of the Crowns under James VI & I

	1606	– Origins of the Guildry
	1608	– Plague epidemic
	1613	– Parish Church galleries erected
	1615	– Rev William Watson leads demonstration by 'Amazone weemen'
	1620	– New Tolbooth completed
	1624	– Severed heads of two pirates put on public display

Charles I became King	– 1625	
	1632 –	Third Royal Burgh Charter
Scottish Coronation of Charles I	– 1633	
	1633 –	Charles I's ferry, the 'Blesing', sank
	1635 –	Death of Lord Melville; East Port built
National Covenant	– 1638	
	1639 –	Rev John Michaelson deposed; West Broomhill fortified
Murder of Archbishop Sharp	– 1639	
English Civil War began	– 1642	
Solemn League & Covenant	– 1643	
	1644 –	Rev John Smith joined Army of the Covenant
	1648 –	Convention of Royal Burghs met in Burntisland because of plague in Edinburgh; three witches burned
Charles I executed; Charles II proclaimed King of Scots	– 1649	
	1649 –	Three witches burned
	1650 –	Unknown number of witches burned
Oliver Cromwell invaded Scotland	– 1650	
Charles II crowned King of Scots at Scone	– 1651	
	1651 –	Oliver Cromwell occupied Burntisland
Charles II fled to France	– 1651	
	1652 –	First horse race to Pettycur (origin of Burntisland Highland Games)
Oliver Cromwell became Lord Protector	– 1653	
Oliver Cromwell died; Richard Cromwell became Lord Protector	– 1658	
Monarchy restored under Charles II	– 1660	
	1660 –	English army of occupation departed
	1665 –	Three women imprisoned for not divulging names of fathers of their children

	1667	Rebel burgesses attempted to overthrow the Town Council
	1671	Star Tavern built
Royal burghs lost monopoly of foreign trade	1672	
	1680	Covenanter David Hackston's body displayed at East Port
	1683	Seven Crafts incorporated
James VII & II became King	1685	
William III and Mary II became King and Queen	1689	
	1689	Rev James Pitcairn assaulted a Kirkcaldy miller
	1692	Town declared bankrupt; some Bailies imprisoned
	1693	Watson's Mortification charity formed
	1699	Rev James Inglis dismissed for his episcopalian beliefs

1707 Union of the Parliaments of Scotland and England

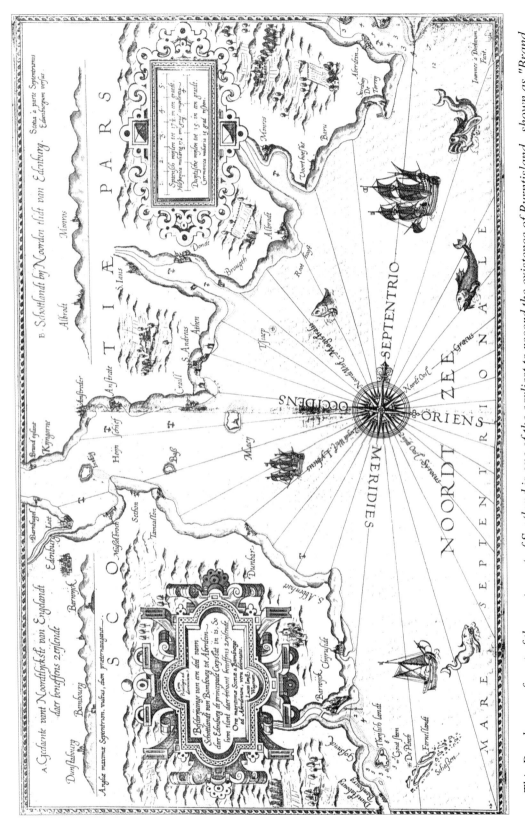

This Dutch map of part of the east coast of Scotland is one of the earliest to record the existence of Burntisland - shown as "Brand eylant" at the top. It was produced by the Dutch hydrographer, L.J. Waghenaer, in 1589. Although it looks wildly inaccurate nowadays, it was in fact a creditable achievement for the era in which it was created. National Library of Scotland.

I Early Times

We can be fairly sure that the advantages of the Burntisland area - an excellent natural harbour, together with the shelter and protection afforded by the Dunearn and Binn Hills to the north- would have made it a favoured choice for settlement from very early times.

This is borne out by a number of significant archaeological discoveries, which confirm that the area has indeed been inhabited for thousands of years.

The cinerary urn discovered in 1866. It is 15 inches high, and 12½ inches in diameter. Kirkcaldy Museum & Art Gallery.

The cup and ring carvings. Fife Council Archaeology Unit.

Andrew Young, writing in 1924, recalled mention of a cairn at the foot of the south face of Craigkennochie, which probably marked a Stoa Age burial site. In the 19th century, the close proximity of this site was blamed for any outbreak of illness in Craigholm Crescent. In 1866, when the foundations of the now demolished Binn House were being dug, a complete cinerary urn (an urn for ashes) containing fragments of charred bone was discovered. This would have held the post-cremation remains of an important person who lived locally some 4,000 years ago.

Several years prior to this find, the Kirke family were using the profits from their sugar plantations in Suriname to build their stately home of Greenmount in Burntisland. During the building work, a number of similar urns were discovered in a stone cist on the site. It may have contained flint arrowheads as well. Unfortunately, these urns were smashed during the building operations.[1]

Much more recently, in 2003, local walkers Colin Kilgour and Jock Moyes realised the significance of rare 'cup and ring' carvings which they had first seen in their childhood. The carvings, on rocks at the foot of the Binn Hill, were examined by archaeologists, who concluded that they would have been created about 4,000 years ago by Bronze Age inhabitants of the Burntisland area.

On the summit of Dunearn Hill to the north-west of the town, there are the remains of a Celtic fort measuring 400 feet by 130 feet, dating from the Early Iron Age (around the 5th century BC). There are also signs of later habitation within the boundaries of the old fort.

---

[1] According to Andrew Young, the broken urns were given to "Mr Paton of Glasgow Museum".

The eminent geographer, Sir Robert Sibbald (1641-1722), identified what he believed to be signs of Roman occupation in the area of Dunearn Hill. He also suggested that Burntisland harbour was used by Agricola, the Roman Governor of Britain, in the year 83 AD, and that there may have been a Roman watchtower and early form of lighthouse where Rossend Castle now stands. There is, however, no extant evidence of these.

Sibbald also mentioned that "some persons in the town, who died not long since, did remember the grassy links reach to the Black-Craig, near a mile into the sea now."

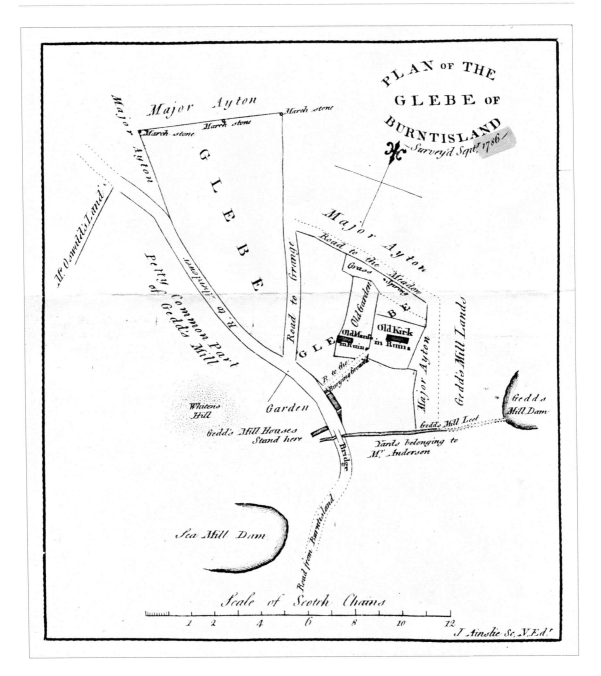

The Kirkton glebe lands in 1786. National Archives of Scotland (RHP 611).

The First Church

We have no idea when our Burntisland forebears became Christians, although we often assume that they were influenced by the great Celtic missionaries from Ireland. But it is quite likely that there were Christians in the area well before that. There is evidence that Roman soldiers and officials who were Christians were in Scotland in the 2nd century. And St Ninian (reputedly educated in Rome) and his followers, based in Whithorn, were active in missionary work from the late 4th century.

Compelling evidence assembled by the Whithorn Trust indicates that St Ninian had links with Charlestown, Dunfermline, Kirkcaldy, St Monance and Pittenweem. Given his apparent enthusiasm for coastal routes and settlements, he is unlikely to have ignored Burntisland on his travels.

The spread of Christianity in Scotland was, however, a piecemeal process, stemming from both Roman and Celtic sources. Even if St Ninian did have some success along the southern coast of Fife, there would be still be much to be done by his follower St Serf (died 583), who was based in Culross from about 520 and was known as the Apostle of West Fife.

These pioneers were followed by St Columba (521-597) and St Adamnan (624-704), both from Ireland. Columba is reputed to have spent some time on Inchcolme island, while Adamnan favoured Inchkeith for study and contemplation. Adamnan was the ninth Abbot of Iona, and his main claim to fame was his writing of Columba's biography.

Burntisland's first known church at the Kirkton is alluded to or mentioned in early records dated 1130, 1184 and 1243, although there may well have been a church there before these dates. 1130 was the year in which King David I granted the lands of Kinghorn Wester to Dunfermline Abbey; and this was confirmed in 1184 by Pope Lucius III.

James Speed records the events of 1243:

17th of May respectively).[2]

The whole parish and its two churches were dedicated to Saint Adamnan, successor of Saint Columba in the office of Abbot of Iona.

The site of the original building is on the east side of Church Street, and is well worth a visit. It contains church ruins and an ancient burying ground. The latest thinking on the visible ruins is that they are of a building which was erected in the first quarter of the 13th century. Some historians have speculated that they might be from a rebuilding in the 15th century, but certain architectural details make this later date unlikely. The simplicity of the chancel arch and the absence of a window in the east wall are architectural features which point to an early 13th century building.

The best preserved part of the church is the eastern section, the chancel. The western section is the nave, and a southern aisle has been added to it. Little of the aisle remains. The small structure to the south east of the aisle is described as a vaulted cell.

The ruins at the Kirkton are of unmistakable architectural and historic importance. They may not be as grand as those elsewhere, but that is part of their charm. They give us an excellent idea of what a simple parish church looked like around the early 13th century.

John Blyth gives us this description of how the Kirkton might have appeared as folk gathered for the Sunday service in the 1500s:

"Before the Reformation and the subsequent erection of the town into a Royal Burgh, the Kirkton and its Church filled an important part in the life of the community. Here, each Sabbath, the inhabitants gathered for public worship - seamen, fishermen, merchants, craftsmen and others, lairds and farm workers, all with their wives and families. Doubtless there was a sprinkling of strangers on many occasions, as, for example, during the period when the French troops of Mary of Lorraine occupied the town, or when some ship from England, France, the Low Countries or the Baltic chanced to lie in the local haven. In the churchyard, after service, would be gathered the usual pedlars and merchants, who were wont to use such occasions to supply the needs of landward folk who had little opportunity to purchase odds and ends of finery, etc. The Roman Church did not frown on this practice, which fitted with the necessities or convenience of olden days, but the Reformation brought an end to such scenes. Inevitably, too, there would be many beggars, deserving and otherwise. The present day Back Causeway or Kirkton Road was then a mere track intercepted at high tide by shallow water, which might have to be crossed by means of stepping stones. Many landward people presumably entered the Churchyard from the Dollar or Dolour Road, which still lies behind the Church."

Rossend Castle

James Speed:
The Castle of Burntisland now called Rossend Castle, is the only ancient building in the immediate neighbourhood of Burntisland. Its early name was the "Tower of Kinghorn Waster" to distinguish it from Glammis Tower or the "Tower of Kinghorne Easter". The exact time of its erection, I believe, cannot now be ascertained. It was probably a Keep or place of refuge in troublous times.

---

[2] This is correct, as the old Julian calendar counts backwards from the Kalends (or first) of the following month.

Top: The ivy covered ruin of the chancel of the Kirkton Church, set against the Binn hill. Iain Sommerville.

Middle: Rossend Castle from the north. Iain Sommerville.

Bottom: Rossend Castle from the east. Ian Archibald.

The picture shows the fine painted ceiling which was inadvertently revealed by rampaging vandals in Rossend Castle in 1957. Until then it had been hidden by a later plaster ceiling. After its discovery, it was dismantled and taken to the National Museum of Antiquities in Edinburgh. It is now on display in the Museum of Scotland in the city.

Towards the bottom left of the picture, on a shield, is the letter 'S', and immediately below it are the initials 'RM'. These almost certainly stand for 'Sir Robert Melville', and place the painting of the ceiling in the period 1594 to 1621. It may have been painted specially for the visit to Burntisland of King James VI & I in 1617.

Like the other Burntisland painted ceilings which are described in Chapter V, the Rossend one is 'tempera', i.e. painted using a mix of ground pigments and glue size. Experts have been unable to detect any unifying philosophical thread connecting the various emblems which are depicted. However, the individual components would each have had their own significance at the time the ceiling was painted.

National Museums of Scotland.

The earliest accounts of it set forth that Durie of that Ilk, Abbot of Dunfermline, built the north and south wings in the year 1382. The armorial bearings of the Duries are inserted in the wall over the principal door. So many of that family were successively Abbots that the house was sometimes called Abbots Hall.

In the Chartulary of Dunfermline Abbey there is recorded a grant of the lands of Nether Grange and Kinghorne Waster together with the keep or fort of the same, and the lands of Erefland and Cunningarland, now Burntisland. This grant is dated 1538. It is probable that though the Duries had long been in the actual possession of these places, they had then for the first time acquired them as private property. At the Reformation the Duries were dispossessed of these lands, and they were bestowed on Sir William Kirkcaldy of Grange, so honourably distinguished as a soldier for his adherence to the Reformation, and for his attachment to the unhappy Queen Mary.

On his death by the hands of the public executioner, these lands appear to have been transferred to the Melvilles of Hall Hill, ancestors of the Earls of Leven and Melville.

St Margaret, wife of Malcolm Canmore, had been buried at Dunfermline. Her remains were collected by King Alexander the III, and the bones placed in a silver chest which at the Reformation was sent to the Castle of Edinburgh and afterwards removed to that of Burntisland by Father Durie.

Queen Mary in her journeys through Fife often lodged here. The apartment which she occupied on these occasions is a wainscoted room in the old square tower and two closets cut out in the wall, which is here ten feet thick. In one of these closets is the entrance to a stair said to have led down to the seashore. The room referred to goes by the name of the State bedchamber.

There is a reference to the "tower portion of Rossend Castle" belonging to the Abbots of Dunfermline in the year 1119, but the source of this information is unknown.

The current owners of Rossend Castle, the Hurd Rolland Partnership, reckon that most of the present building dates from the mid 16th century. However, they also believe that a section of the west wing was built in the 13th century. This section contains parts of three lancet windows.

Speed mentioned St Margaret's relics. Some commentators have suggested that her skull, with auburn hair still attached, and some other bones were placed in a magnificent silver chest decorated with gold and encrusted with precious stones, and that this chest was concealed in Burntisland (later Rossend) Castle for over 30 years until 1597, when they were taken to the continent. Recent investigations by local historian Bruce Durie throw doubt on this claim, although there is some evidence that it might be true.

Expanding on Speed's reference to Mary, Queen of Scots, we can recount the fascinating tale of the over-amorous Frenchman, Chastellard, and his tragic end.

Mary was spending the night of the 14th of February, 1562, in Rossend Castle, when she had a surprise visitor. An anonymous 19th century writer takes up the story:

"The romantic Frenchman, Chastellard, repeated the misdemeanour of which he had been previously guilty at Holyrood, of concealing himself in the Queen's sleeping chamber at night. Desperate in his attachment, he had secretly followed the Queen to Burntisland, and gaining an entrance to the Castle by the unfrequented staircase, he started from his hiding-place when the Queen was in the act of retiring to bed.

Queen Mary's bedchamber in Rossend Castle. Alan Barker Collection.

The shrieks of the Queen and her attendant women brought assistance. Mary, glowing with indignation at the insult, commanded Moray, who first ran to her succour, to stab him with his dagger, but he preferring securing him to this summary vengeance, a formal trial followed, and the miserable man was condemned and executed within two days after his offence.

On the scaffold, instead of having recourse to his missal or breviary, he drew from his pocket a volume of Ronsard, and, reciting the poet's hymn to Death, resigned himself to his fate with gaiety and indifference. Ascending the scaffold erected before the windows of Holyrood[3], the theatre of his madness and the dwelling of the Queen, he faced death like a hero and a poet. Then casting his last looks towards the windows of the Palace inhabited by the charm of his life and the cause of his death, he cried 'Farewell, thou who art so beautiful and so cruel, who killest me, and whom I cannot cease to love.' "

According to Andrew Young, the staircase mentioned in this account led from outside the Queen's bedchamber via the castle scullery to a secret passageway to the shore. Building excavations at the west end of the High Street in the mid 19th century did indeed expose an arched passageway - six feet underground and four feet in height - but no further exploration was made and the hole was filled in.

There has, however, been no evidence to support stories of another underground passage from the castle - in this case running to Dunearn House via the Grange, a distance of nearly one and a half miles.

What's in a Name?

<u>James Speed</u>:
The name of Burntisland is of uncertain derivation. The latter part of the word has been imagined to be derived from the almost insular position of the town, or from the island which forms the south west boundary of the harbour. Amongst the various ways in which the word has been successively written are Byrtland, Byrtiland, Bruntiland, Burntisland. Part of the ground ..... was anciently called Erefland and Cunningarland or rabbit warren. In the several charters of the Burgh the harbour is called "Portus Gratiae" and "Portus Salutis".

Local historians have had great fun speculating on the derivation of the town's rather curious name, but have not had much success in finding the answer. This includes Robert Livingstone, who discovered 20 or more spelling variations in old documents. Of course, such

---

[3] Other sources say he was executed at St Andrews.

variations were not uncommon in the old days, when handwriting could easily be misread or the spoken word transcribed as it sounded rather than according to any spelling rules.

Burntisland may well be the anglicised version of the Scots form, 'Bruntiland', which means quite simply a burnt island. (Andrew Young sounds a note of caution, though, pointing out that some of the earlier references in old documents are to 'Bertiland'.)

The favoured choice for the island is the one sometimes known as the Green Island. It is now part of the site occupied by Burntisland Fabrications Ltd, and before that, the shipyard.

The usual explanation for 'burnt' is that there were at one time fishermen's huts on the Green Island, and that these were destroyed by fire.

An alternative suggestion has been that the name is derived from the Scots 'Bruntland' (rough ground, burnt periodically). This is the explanation favoured by Douglas Speirs, Fife Council's archaeologist.

Unfortunately, it is unlikely that we will ever have a definitive explanation, although the simple 'burnt island' one will continue to be the most popular.

The Green Island can be seen clearly in this aerial view of Burntisland Harbour. It is indicated by the white arrow, and stretches from the bottom right corner of the buildings on the left to the north end of the harbour wall. Crown copyright RCAHMS.

II Burgh Charters and Boundaries

The plaque on the pillar at the entrance to Burntisland Links tells us that they were 'Granted to the Burgh by Royal Charter of James V - June 1541'. The charter itself, the original of which is now held in the National Archives of Scotland in Edinburgh, confirms that Burntisland was indeed granted Royal Burgh status in 1541. However, as we shall see, it was not until 1585-86 that Burntisland was able to adopt all the rights and responsibilities of a royal burgh.

If a community in Scotland was elevated to burgh status, it would gain a degree of self government. Without burgh status, it would typically remain at the beck and call of the local aristocratic landowner.

There were different classes of burgh, and at the top of the scale was the royal burgh, which enjoyed extensive privileges. Royal burgh status was definitely something to aspire to. James Speed has provided us with a helpful description of the background to the establishment of royal burghs in Scotland, and the full version can be seen in Appendix A. The following is an extract.

James Speed:

Burghs of Regality and Barony - besides the Burghs Royal, there were Burghs erected by Lords of Regality and Barons, called respectively Burghs of Regality and Baron Burghs and governed by Magistrates appointed by them. The inhabitants of these places had few privileges which the rural inhabitants did not possess and the authority of their Magistrates was limited to petty cases either civil or criminal.

[Burntisland] harbour and the adjoining territory were the property of the Abbot and Monks of Dunfermline Abbey; and the town existed as a burgh of Regality under them in the year 1506, but how long before that time I have not been able to discover.

In the year 1541 James the fifth gave certain lands to George, Archdeacon of St. Andrews and Commendator of Dunfermline, in exchange for the harbour of Burntisland and "sax acres" of land adjoining thereto, and erected them into a Burgh Royal. The town was proclaimed as a Burgh Royal with the customary solemnities in the year 1568. But the possession of its privileges seems to have been successfully opposed by the Commendator of Dunfermline. It is indeed uncertain if it ever fully enjoyed them, for in the year 1574 a charter erecting it into a Burgh of Regality, passing over the first Royal charter without notice, was granted by the Commendator, Lord Robert Pitcairn.

According to James Speed, Burntisland had become a burgh of regality prior to 1506. In 1541, King James V promoted Burntisland to royal burgh. In the charter which he granted in that year, he referred to the development work on the harbour which he had commissioned and paid for, and the desirability of the town itself also being developed quickly. Royal burgh status was intended to help this process.

However, both the church and the aristocracy were in general opposed to the creation of royal burghs. The lands given to the royal burghs typically came from them. As the royal burghs grew in number and strength, the church and the aristocracy, as well as losing land, also lost an equivalent degree of political influence. Burntisland was by no means the only royal burgh to have problems with the church and local landowners.

The Royal Charter of 1541, granted by King James V. National Archives of Scotland (C 2/31/8).

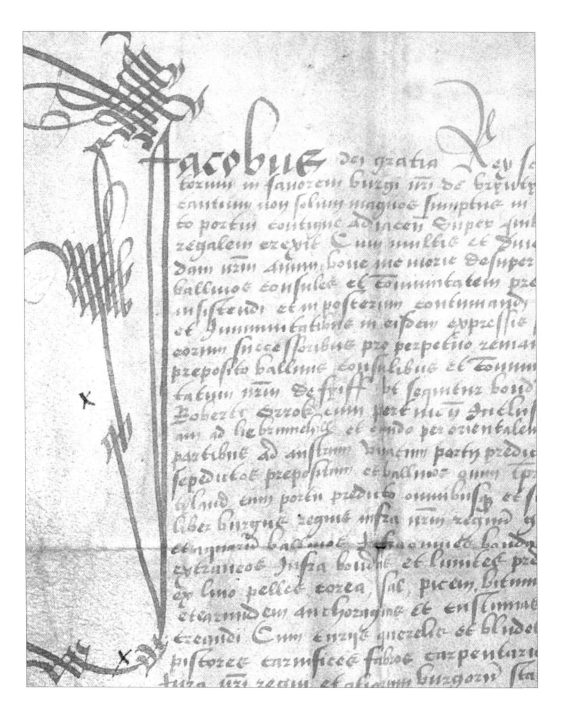

An extract from the Royal Charter of 1585, granted by King James VI.
This gives a good idea of the type of handwriting used at the time.
National Archives of Scotland (B 9/14/2).

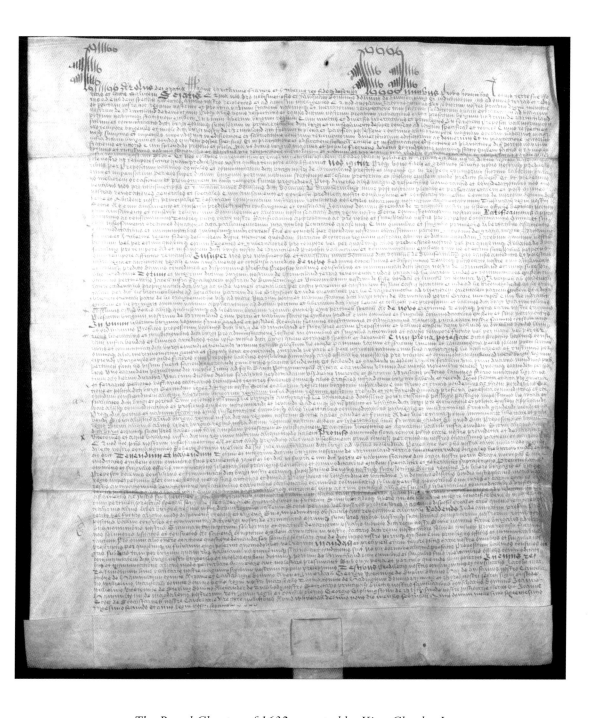

The Royal Charter of 1632, granted by King Charles I.
National Archives of Scotland (B 9/14/3).

In Burntisland's case, it was the church authorities based in Dunfermline who had lost their land, and it was the church which threw a spanner in the works and cast Burntisland into a state of limbo for over 40 years.

The problem which allowed the church to intervene was likely to have been that the charter of 1541 had not been ratified by the Scottish Parliament. Burntisland was only half way to being a royal burgh, and the church made sure that the town did not function as one.

During this rather confusing period, King James VI granted Burntisland a further charter in 1573, confirming the town in its earlier status as a burgh of regality. No doubt the leading citizens of the town would have looked on this as being better than nothing, but the campaign for confirmation of royal burgh status was not abandoned.

In 1583, Burntisland applied to the Convention of Burghs for inclusion as a royal burgh, but a decision was deferred. However, success came in 1585, when James VI granted the town a new charter, confirming that of 1541 and stating unequivocally that Burntisland was a free royal burgh. Most importantly, the charter was granted "with consent of the Parliament of Scotland".

James Speed:

New Royal Charter. In the year 1585 a new Royal Charter was obtained substantially the same as that of 1541; but on this occasion confirmed by act of Parliament. This Charter sets forth that King James the sixth having found that his ancestor King James the fifth as a reward for the gratuitous services rendered to him and his predecessors, Kings of Scotland, by the inhabitants of Byrtiland since its erection into a great civil community "and to encourage them to go forward in increasing their numbers and in prosecuting trade and navigation, had at great expense constructed the port called the Port of Grace, and disposed it and the lands adjoining thereto acquired from the Abbots and Monks of Dunfermline to the provost, Bailies, Council and community thereof, and erected these lands into a free Royal Burgh with all the liberties, privileges and immunities granted or to be granted to such institutions all things non nominate being to be held as nominate as well above the earth as under the earth far off as at hand therefore renews and confirms the said Charter of erection."

Boundaries. The boundaries of the Burgh, as described in both Charters, begin at the west bulwark, now called the half moon, on the west from the point passing under the fortalice of Burntisland, now called Rossend Castle eastward, and then passing to the Broom Hill and going by the weather glow thereof to Greigshole, thence by Craigkennoquhy to the sea, together with the port called the Port of Grace.

In case anyone was in any doubt, there was a subsequent 'Ratification by King James the VI, with the consent of Parliament, of different Grants and Charters in favour of the Burgh of Burntisland', dated 29 July 1587.

The granting of the charter of 1585 and the ratification of 1587 should have been the end of the matter. However, the church authorities based in Dunfermline still felt aggrieved at the loss of their valuable land, and continued to pursue their case for its return.

Their anti-Burntisland stance attracted an ally in Sir Robert Melville, the new occupier of Rossend Castle, who laid claim to the burgh land between his castle and the sea. Sir Robert had another item on his agenda too, for he owned the Sea Mills in what is now the Red Pond area. Sir Robert claimed that the folk in Burntisland had a legal obligation (termed thirlage) to bring all their grain to his mills for grinding. This was in direct contradiction of the terms of the 1585 burgh charter, which vested in the burgh the powers to regulate its own trade.

Above: The Sea Mill by Andrew Young (1921). Collection of the late Cathy Watson.

Below: View to the West by Andrew Young (1912), in Burntisland Burgh Chambers. What was then a hay field is now Broomhill Avenue and Dick Crescent. Ian Archibald.

"Burnt Island, Fifeshire" by S. Humble (1836). This oil painting is on display in the Magistrates' Room of Burntisland Burgh Chambers. It shows how the south and east of the town looked prior to the arrival of the railway. It also appears to show part of the old town walls. Iain Sommerville.

Melville was a shrewd political operator. He got himself elected Provost of Burntisland from 1588 to 1599, from 1604 to 1606, and again from 1618 to 1632. It may seem surprising that he was elected by the Town Council with whom he was in dispute - but he was able to use his influence at Court and among the rich and famous to bring irresistible pressure to bear on the ordinary town councillors.

Sir Robert inherited the title Lord Melville on the death of his father in 1621.

James Speed:
[In 1606 the] Earl of Dunbar was again elected Provost, and promised to do his best to defeat the renewed attempts of Sir Robert Melville and his Lady, Lady Ross, to get the town disfranchised. The cause of this new attempt on the liberties of the Burgh was the continued opposition of the inhabitants to the thirlage of the Sea Mills. On this occasion, in order to propitiate Sir Robert and his Lady, the Council resolved "to treat them with courtesy and wait on them on Sundays at the Castle gate, and accompany them to the Kirk". The Bishop of Brechin ..... was mediator on this occasion; but neither the courtesy of the Council nor the mediation of the Bishop had the desired effect.

So worried were the Town Council of the Royal Burgh of Burntisland by this constant harassment that they appealed to King Charles I for yet another charter. This was granted in 1632 and ratified by Parliament in 1633. It confirmed for the third time that Burntisland was a royal burgh.

It had been intended to keep this application secret until everything had been signed and sealed, to prevent Melville from interfering and trying to influence the King. But he got wind of what was going on, and demanded concessions.

The Town Council therefore agreed to issue a statement acknowledging Melville's objection to the provisions of the charter. However, there would be no change to the charter itself, which confirmed that the burgh's land included the disputed area between Rossend Castle and the sea. And the Town Council refused point blank to budge on the Sea Mills issue. Melville had effectively been defeated.

The church authorities in Dunfermline and the owners of Rossend Castle continued to grumble about their lost lands for many years, but for all practical purposes the granting of the charter of 1632 meant the end of the matter.

Lord Melville died in 1635. With heavy irony, Speed notes: "The Council and 'honest men' of the Burgh were appointed to 'ride' at Lord Melville's funeral at Monimail. They would be greatly grieved no doubt, considering how true a friend they had lost."

Burgh Seals and Arms

It was common practice for Scottish burghs to adopt a seal, which was usually a circular relief moulding comprising a depiction of an appropriate object - in Burntisland's case, a ship - surrounded by a caption. The original function of the seal was to validate important documents by adding to them the imprint of the seal in sealing wax.

In due course, the seal took on an additional function and its design was used as a decorative addition to buildings and other structures - in the same way as a burgh coat of arms was used in more recent years.

Top left: a very old copy of the seal of the Royal Burgh of Burntisland, probably dating from the late 16th century. National Museums of Scotland.

Top right: the Burgh seal carved in stone on the wall of the old courthouse in Links Place. Iain Sommerville.

Middle: the ornate version of the Burgh seal in the Burgh Chambers. Iain Sommerville.

Bottom: the Arms of the Royal Burgh of Burntisland from a painted panel in the Parish Church. Gavin Anderson.

James Speed tells us that, in 1597, "A Common Seal was adopted, having on it the figure of King James V in full armour, no doubt as an expression of gratitude for having conferred on the town the status of a Burgh Royal."

Unfortunately, there is no trace of the seal described by Speed, although Andrew Young speculated that it might have been the coket seal, which was used in customs procedures at the port.

The Royal Burgh of Burntisland certainly had its own municipal seal for very many years. The version pictured top left on page 30 has been dated by the National Musums of Scotland as likely to be late 16th century. It may be that Speed was correct with the date of 1597, but got the description wrong.

The old burgh seal is still visible in the town. A badly eroded version is on the wall of the old burgh court (now the Unity Hall) in Links Place; and it can also be seen on the 19th century fountain at the entrance to the Links. There is a painted copy on the canopy of the Magistrates' Seat in the Parish Church. A much grander version is above the door of the Magistrates' Room in the Burgh Chambers.

The seal emphasises Burntisland's role as a port, and shows a three masted vessel on the sea, with sails furled, flags flying, and two mariners on board. The Latin text encircling the picture is "SIGILLUM BURGI DE BRUNTISLAND", meaning simply "Seal of the Burgh of Burntisland". It is said that the reverse side of one version of the seal carried a picture of a fish, probably a herring, and the words "Success to the Herring Fishing". The Common Seal, that used for endorsing documents, had nothing on the reverse.

In the 1930s, the Town Council decided that Burntisland should have its own coat of arms, and in 1938 the Lord Lyon King of Arms granted the arms which are illustrated on page 30. R.M. Urquhart gives the following description: "The arms repeat the device on the Burgh seal, a device said to have been used by Burntisland for centuries. The ship refers to the town's long history as a seaport and its connection in more modern times with shipbuilding. The red and gold colours of Fife are used ..... Two mottoes were allowed: 'Portus Gratiae' ..... was the name given to the place by the Romans because of its safe harbour; the other motto (also in Latin) - 'God gave the hills for protection' - was suggested by Mr. A. Wishart, W.S., of Edinburgh, who was a native of Burntisland parish and an authority on its history. The hills referred to in the motto are Dunearn and The Binn, which guard the town to the North."

When Burntisland Town Council was wound up in 1975 on the reorganisation of local government, the coat of arms could no longer be used. Burntisland Community Council therefore applied to the Lord Lyon for the grant of new arms for its own use, and these were awarded in 1997. They are similar to those of the old town council.

It is also worth noting here the existence of a version of the Royal Arms, which is probably around 370 years old and is mounted on the wall of the Court Room in the Burgh Chambers. Robert Livingstone looked into the history of this painted wooden sculpture, and concluded that it dated from around the visit of King Charles I in 1633. He traced its movements as follows. From about 1633 to 1843 it was housed in the tolbooth at the foot of the High Street. Until 1886 it was stored in the belfry of the new Burgh Chambers. In 1886 it was moved to the old court house in Links Place, where it was painted over. It was rediscovered in 1954, restored by a local painter, and hung in the Burgh Chambers where it remains to this day.

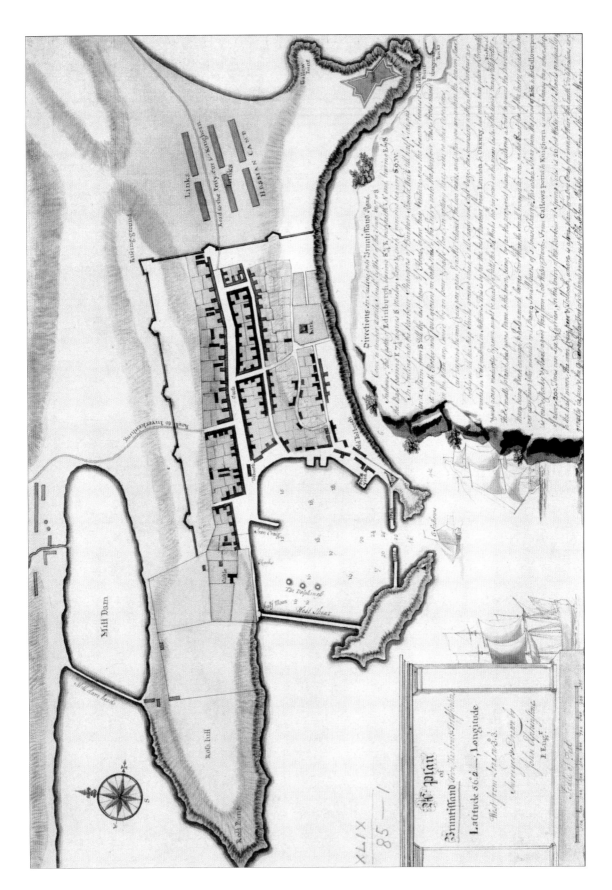

On the opposite page: map of Burntisland in 1746 by James Elphinstone, military engineer. The Hessian troops (mercenaries from Hesse in Germany) who were camped on the Links had been hired by the Government to help quell the Jacobite rebellion of 1745-46. The north and east town walls are clearly marked. At the bottom right are instructions for sailing into Burntisland roads. British Library.

On this page: the north and east town walls from Elphinstone's map are superimposed on a relatively recent aerial photograph of the town. The broken red line indicates where possible west and south walls might have been, although the cliffs and the sea would by themselves have provided substantial protection. Crown Copyright RCAHMS.

III   The Town Council and the State

In the previous chapter, we learned something of the difficulties which our municipal ancestors had in establishing Burntisland as a royal burgh. So what exactly were they fighting for?

James Speed:
[The benefits from] the full establishment and recognition of the town as a Royal Burgh [were] personal freedom in some considcrable respects; the rights of local government; of trading; of holding corporate property; of Parliamentary representation and other rights; [which] sufficiently account for the earnestness with which the community contended for their independence.
..... Besides the ground on which the town is built, the Royalty includes the Links, the Broom Hills, and the Lammerlaws. The Burgesses have the privilege of using the Links for grazing cattle. It is also used as a place of exercise, for playing golf and other games. It is of very great value to the inhabitants and with the Broom Hills and Craigkennoquhy, is secured in perpetuity to them as a place of recreation.

The prize was to join the elite of Scottish communities, and enjoy self government in the management of most of the town's affairs. As Christopher Smout put it, a royal burgh was a "state within a state".

According to Robert Livingstone's research, Burntisland was the seventeenth Scottish royal burgh to be created. Although this figure has been disputed, it is likely that Burntisland was indeed a relatively early recipient of the honour, which placed it in a privileged position compared to most of the Scotland's communities. In the 17th century, there were between 60 and 70 royal burghs in Scotland.

In return for its royal charter, Burntisland had to take on certain obligations - for example, the collection of national taxes and levies, and the provision of recruits (willing or otherwise) for the army and navy.

However, Burntisland and the other royal burghs were by no means models of democracy. Self government effectively meant government by the burgesses. The Town Council decided who should or should not become a burgess. Applicants had to be men of substance, as James Speed shows in the following extract.

James Speed:
Burgesses and Freemen paid on their admission from ten merks to thirty pounds scots each, according to their supposed ability, and gave a banquet to the council sometimes called "the spice and wine". The banquet seemed never to be omitted. Freemen's eldest sons were admitted gratis, always excepting the banquet. The new Burgess afterwards appeared in the Burgh court and swore to be faithful to the king; to defend the liberties of the Burgh; and to assist the Magistrates in the due execution of their duty. He required to be of good moral character; of the true religion, able to bear the king's fine; to reside, bear scot and lot, and watch and ward when required; and be owner of a rood of bigget land. Non-residents were held to be honorary only, though their names appeared in the list of Burgesses.

Speed was convinced that Burntisland was a burgh of regality by 1506, so there would have been some sort of town council in existence by that date. There were certainly bailies in post at the time of the charter of 1573. We know that Burgh Court books from 1582 survive in the National Archives of Scotland. After exhaustive research, Robert Livingstone concluded that the Town Council of the Royal Burgh of Burntisland probably first met in 1586, the year after the granting of the charter of 1585. John Clapen, a local shipmaster, was appointed the first Provost on 10 October 1586. He was clearly a man of some standing, because 23 years earlier he had received a "Certificate of Character" from the court of Mary, Queen of Scots.

The actual mechanics via which Burntisland became a burgh of regality, and subsequently a royal burgh, are unclear. It is likely that the King would have appointed one or more reeves (stewards) to supervise the process and get the first town councils up and running.

In the 17th century, the leading burgesses in Burntisland would be the merchants, shipowners and shipmasters. In theory, any permanent resident could aspire to become a burgess, and so share in the government of the burgh and gain certain other privileges. However, as the requirements included the ownership of land, the payment of an entrance fee, and the provision of lavish hospitality, only the better off folk qualified.

We do not know how many burgesses there were in Burntisland in the early years, although the number would be relatively small. (In 1835, there were 75 burgesses resident in the town, of whom only 31 were eligible for election to the council.)

In Burntisland, as in other royal burghs, succeeding town councils were elected by the retiring members, again from among the burgesses. The retiring and new members then jointly appointed the principal officebearers, listed below by James Speed. This system allowed a small number of families to control the affairs of a burgh for long periods.

Periodically there would be general meetings of a burgh's leading citizens, called Head Courts, to give those citizens the opportunity to influence the council. In Burntisland, the Head Courts were held up until about 1800. James Speed reckoned that their influence was significant.

James Speed:
[Burntisland town] council consisted of twenty one members including a provost, who was almost always a nobleman or landed gentleman. He was considered the patron of the burgh and was expected to support its interests by his influence. [There were also] three bailies, treasurer and procurator fiscal. The other office men were a common clerk, who was some times a Councillor, three constables, Quartermasters to call out the inhabitants to watch and ward or for military service; and two town's officers dressed in the town's livery - that was "four tailed red coats with white lining".

..... Disputes having arisen as to the manner of electing the Council, the whole matter was in 1732 referred to arbitration. By the decreet issued on that occasion the council was to consist, as before, of twenty one person[s], of whom fourteen, including all the Magistrates, were to be guild brethren, and seven craftsmen, one of each craft. A Dean of Guild was also appointed with six assessors. Each craft chose its own Deacon, but he had no place in the Council. All the other office-bearers were chosen by the Council. The old council chose the new. The community had no direct voice in the matter.

..... The municipal constitution of Burntisland was substantially the same as that of the other Burghs of Scotland during that time. The internal government of these places was in many respects very defective, and led to great abuses. As a whole, however the existence of these incorporations was conducive to the maintenance of civil and religious liberty during the tumults of the seventeenth century. The privileges of the Burgesses gave them a greater degree of influence in national affairs than was possessed by the corresponding class of landward people.

..... After the union with England, the elective franchise for the Burghs was vested in the Town Councils, and was a chief cause why the Burgh system was maintained entire long after its defects were seen and acknowledged by all parties. ..... It therefore remained ..... till it was entirely removed by the passing of the Burgh Reform Act of 1833.

By this Act the Burgesses were deprived of their peculiar privileges, and their interest in the corporate property was transferred to others. Thus for the public benefit they were virtually extinguished as a class, for the word Burgess is now only an empty name.[4] This act has been followed by many beneficial consequences. The station, however, of Burgh Magistrates has since that time declined.

On at least one occasion, there was an attempt to overthrow Burntisland Town Council by direct action, rather than through the normal - but distinctly undemocratic - procedures. In 1667, a group of disenchanted burgesses arranged unauthorised public meetings, elected their own representatives, and went as far as levying their own taxes. The leaders of the uprising were five seamen, two maltmen, a merchant and a cooper. The revolution was short lived, and two of the leaders ended up in Edinburgh Tolbooth.

The post of provost was left unfilled in the period from 1633 to 1689. The reason for this may have been that Lord (formerly Sir Robert) Melville of Rossend Castle had been provost for the preceding 15 years. At that time he had been no friend of the burgh, as we saw in Chapter II, but he had used his influence to gain the provostship - no doubt hoping to convert the Town Council to his way of thinking. The charter of 1632 effectively ended Melville's campaign against the burgh, and the Town Council may have been keen to avoid risking a repetition of the problems caused by having a provost with a personal and anti-burgh agenda. The easiest solution would have been to avoid having a provost at all.

For its size, Burntisland had a relatively large town council of 21 members. By comparison, the city of Perth had only twelve. Given the small number of burgesses in the town, it was sometimes difficult to fill all the places on the council. This was also the case at times such as Cromwell's occupation, when unpopular laws had to be implemented or harsh taxes collected.

Burntisland Town Council had many important responsibilities, and we deal with some of these in more detail in later chapters.

James Speed:
There was ..... a jury of fifteen persons appointed by the Council 'to make the statutes', mainly to prescribe at what price Ale, Wine, Meal, Candles and some other things were to be sold. Bread was ordained to be sold at so many ounces for each twelve pennies Scotch. This weight varied from 14 to 17 ounces. This jury also determined how much of each hundred pounds of direct taxes, whether for national or local purposes, each inhabitant had to pay.

---

[4] The title of burgess was in fact used on a very small number of occasions in later years, when Burntisland Town Council wished to grant the freedom of the burgh to deserving individuals by making them Honorary Burgesses. One such was Andrew Carnegie in 1907. The last occasion was in 1975, just before the abolition of town councils, when three persons were so honoured.

The business of the Council was conducted with much attention to regularity. Prayers were said at the opening and close of each meeting. Members were required to come in 'honest hats and cloaks, and not in bonnets and other unseemly wear'. Meetings were held weekly at eight o'clock in the morning. Those absent or departing before the last prayer were fined in twelve shillings scots. All were required 'to sit gravely and in silence till their opinion or vote was required by the Moderator'. Strict secrecy was required. Those who used profane language were to be fined in thirty shillings; obstinate transgressors were to be expelled the Council. Such were the rules, but the records show that they were but indifferently obeyed.

The council's ability to enforce its regulations on trade and other matters was helped enormously by the fact that Burntisland was a walled town. The walls are shown on the map on page 32, and on the photograph on page 33. Although the map is dated 1746, the walls shown would have been in existence for many years before that.

Until 1689, the Scottish Parliament was made up of representatives of the nobility, the church and the royal burghs, who sat together in a single chamber. In 1690, the church representatives were replaced by representatives of the counties. As a royal burgh, Burntisland was always represented, and therefore able to participate in discussions on national issues. Speed tells us that, in 1597, Burntisland was sending two Commissioners to Parliament. The town was also represented in the powerful Convention of Royal Burghs.

James Speed gives the following example of the Town Council's mandating of its Parliamentary Commissioner in 1700.

James Speed:
1700. The council instructed Bailie Ged to vote in Parliament.
1st - For securing the Protestant religion as established by law;
2nd - That the settlement of Darien was a rightful and lawful establishment, and to consent to the granting of a supply for carrying it on;
3rd - For a reduction of forces and for a supply suitable thereto;
4th - For rectifying grievances; and
5th - For making such laws as shall conduce to the welfare of the king and kingdom.

On 16 January 1707, the Scottish Parliament ratified the Act of Union by 110 votes to 67, and Scotland and England united. Despite the fact that the royal burghs were being allowed to retain their special status, most of them voted against the Act.

Burntisland lost its direct representation in Parliament, and had to be content with sharing a single Member of Parliament with Kinghorn, Kirkcaldy and Dysart in the new Dysart Burghs constituency. Worse still, the Union signalled a serious reduction in trade for the Fife ports. Burntisland was badly affected, and many years would pass before there was an improvement. This may have been the reason for the increased support which the Jacobite cause enjoyed locally in the post Union years.

The Tolbooth, the Tron and the Market Cross

No self-respecting royal burgh would be without three essential structures.

The first was the tolbooth, which usually provided some working space for the town's employees, and also a jail in which to confine the law breakers. The second was the tron house (or cross house), which housed the public weighing machine (the tron). The tron house was usually adjacent to the third structure, the market cross, which marked the spot where the traders were entitled to display their wares on the appointed market days. Although termed a cross, its form varied from town to town. It had other functions too, as we see in the illustration below.

The position of Burntisland's first tolbooth was close to what is now Forth Place. It must have still been standing in 1746, because it is clearly marked on the map on page 32.

The position of the new tolbooth, built between 1613 and 1620, is shown on the same map, as is the market cross. The position of the cross is today indicated by a cobbled marker on the carriageway of the High Street, just to the west of the public library. Excavations in this area in 1912 revealed the cut sandstone foundations of a small circular building, 14 feet in diameter. It is likely that the building was Burntisland's tron house.

Thanks to James Speed, Andrew Young and John Blyth, we know something of the history of the new tolbooth. Andrew Young was able to draw a picture of it, based on old records and folk memories. His drawing is reproduced on the front cover.

Initially, this building had seven booths for local traders on the ground floor. Examples of the tenants were a baker, a brewer and a butcher.

Speed tells us that "On the first floor of the tower were wretched cells for criminal prisoners, and two small rooms above for debtors - places in which no human being could long retain health of either mind or body. A large hall and a court and council room occupied the west part of the building."

Janet Haldane in 1656, ordered to stand at the cross with 'A VILE SLANDERER' inscribed on a paper on her head. Pen and ink drawing by Ian McLeod.

Because the Burntisland ferry was the main link between Edinburgh and the north, the town's tolbooth was also used as a short term holding station for prisoners who were being transported in either direction. There is a particularly distressing story of such use for Covenanter prisoners, which is told in Chapter IV.

On a more light-hearted note, Andrew Young recounts memories of the often lenient treatment afforded to local folk who had been locked in the cells. The Town Officer would turn a blind eye when a prisoner let down a rope from his cell window, so that a few luxury items could be unofficially supplied by family and friends. On one occasion, an incarcerated debtor gave the Town Officer half a crown to get him a bottle of whisky. While the officer was on his errand, the prisoner escaped. Needless to say, the Town Officer lost his job.

The tolbooth sported useful accessories, such as the town bell, bought second hand from Berwick in 1619. There was also a prominent town clock on the east gable, facing the High Street.

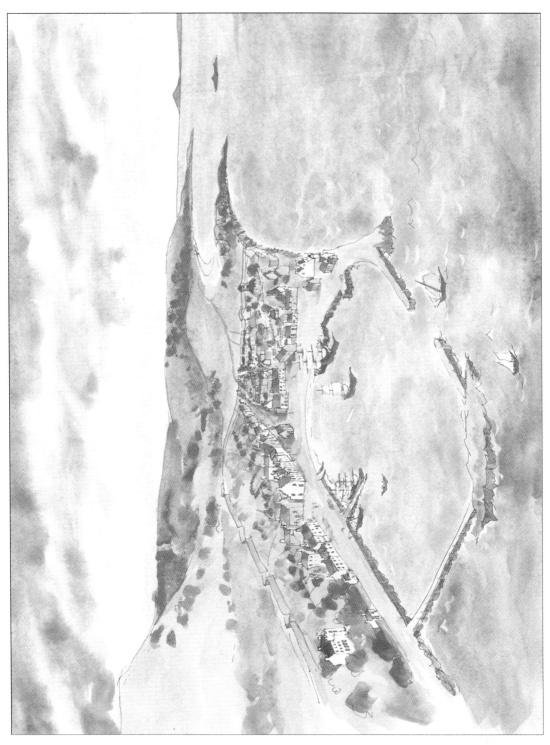

On the right: Old Burntisland viewed from the west. Watercolour by Keli Clark.

On the opposite page: The East Port by Andrew Young. Burntisland Heritage Trust Collection.

41

The 1620 tolbooth served the town well for over 200 years, although latterly it attracted much criticism. Provost Farnie described it as "that abominable old court house". Its fate was sealed in the 1840s, with the completion of the Prince Albert pier and of the new road to Kinghorn. Impediments to the free movement of traffic had to go. And so, in 1843, Burntisland lost its old tolbooth and also its East Port - demolished in the name of progress. The tolbooth was replaced in 1846 by the fine new town house at the corner of High Street and Kirkgate. The Prince Albert pier itself did not have a long life, as its site was required for the East Dock, which opened in 1901.

The town drummer beat his drum daily through the town at seven o'clock in the morning and four o'clock in the afternoon. There was also a town violer who played a stringed instrument, a precursor of the violin. Speed notes that he complained that violers living outside the Burgh came in and played on 'bass and triple viols to his prejudice' - so they were banned.

Burntisland's Town Drummer. His job was to alert the inhabitants when something important was about to happen. Drawing by Douglas Gray.

Taxation

When a town became a royal burgh, it had to accept the obligations as well as the privileges. The principal obligations were the acceptance of responsibility for paying a share of national direct taxes, and for supplying recruits (volunteers or conscripts) for the national army and navy.

Local authorities today are always complaining about 'lack of resources', i.e. money. But they have it relatively easy compared with the hand to mouth existence of a small royal burgh like Burntisland in the 17th century.

Regular national taxation in Scotland began in the 1580s. The amount to be raised was agreed by the Scottish Parliament, which comprised the 'three estates' of nobles, clergy and royal burghs. The collection of the royal burghs' share was delegated to the Convention of Royal Burghs.

The Convention based the levies on individual burghs on their ability to pay, and Speed has given us some comparative figures for the year 1670. In that year, Burntisland was liable for 1.15% of the total to be raised from the royal burghs. Speed also quoted examples of levies on other burghs, to allow us to compare how wealthy Burntisland was in relation to them - Edinburgh 33.67%, Glasgow 31.00%, Aberdeen 7.00%, Perth 3.85%, Cupar 1.00%, Dunfermline 0.80%, Dysart 0.80%, Kinghorn 0.45%, Inverkeithing 0.40%, Inverbervie 0.05%, North Berwick 0.05%.

In the levying of taxes, the Convention's treatment of individual burghs varied considerably - although in general it had a reputation for leniency if presented with a hard luck story. James Speed gives us the following two examples of its treatment of Burntisland - one where the Convention took a hard line, and one where it was so generous that the decision had to be kept secret.

<u>James Speed</u>:
c1687. The inhabitants were in great distress at this time owing to the losses sustained by the capture of many of their ships during the war with Holland, and the expense they were subjected to for the maintenance of soldiers and prisoners quartered on the town, and in transporting them to Leith. A representation on the subject having been made, the Earl of Balcarras, in place of giving relief, intimated that unless the government assessments were paid, he would quarter more troops on the town - no vain threat as the inhabitants knew by experience. Therefore, to prevent the entire ruin of the town, the Council, after various expedients had been tried, borrowed money from the Kirk Session, Prime [Gilt] and private persons, till their credit was exhausted, to enable them to pay the tax or so much of it as could not be collected from the inhabitants.

..... c1690. Quartering. The oppressive and tyrannical custom of quartering soldiers on the inhabitants to compel them to pay the government taxes was continued under the Revolution government in the same way as under that of the Steuarts. The Council applied to the Lord High Commissioner for relief on account of the poverty of the town and because of the debt due to it by government for the expense of transporting soldiers from the north. Relief was at first refused, but afterwards some alleviation was obtained by the influence of Lord Raith, but secretly, "as such a favour had not been granted to any Burgh".

It was the responsibility of Burntisland Town Council to find the money to pay the national taxes, and also to carry out any local projects which they wanted to undertake. Personal taxes were levied on the better off members of the community. In addition, the town received revenue from various other levies and duties - from which, according to Speed, the following sums were raised in the year 1623:

Anchorage	200 pounds Scots
Import on Ale	50 pounds Scots
Small Customs	50 pounds Scots
Boat Silver	41 pounds Scots
Duty on Hired Horses	143 pounds Scots
Total	**484 pounds Scots**

The Town Council would sometimes raise money for specific purposes. For example, Speed tells us that, around 1681, "Twelve pennies were exacted by order of the Council for each load of coals brought into the town, to be applied towards the expense of causewaying the streets. This tax continued for many years."

In the 1640s, Burntisland Town Council is reported as having tried to avoid the collection of the very unpopular excise duty on behalf of Parliament. Their imaginative excuse was that they could find no-one prepared to accept appointment as Collector. Parliament responded by demanding that, if no-one would accept appointment, the town councillors should collect the duty themselves.

On rare occasions, the Council might have to find the ransom for a local lad who was being held in a far off land: "1674. ..... A letter was received from Inverkeithing with a copy of an act of the Privy Council, authorizing a contribution for the ransom of three sailors detained by the Turks in Salec, of whom one belonged to Burntisland. The ransom was said to be 500 or 600 dollars for each. The Council authorised the contribution, and desired the minister to intimate it from the pulpit."

In the late 1680s, Burntisland was facing a financial crisis. Speed reports a rather suspicious tidying up of the books in 1689: "At this time, as if there had been a fear of investigation, there were clearings up of accounts and giving discharges to those who had been concerned in the administration of Burghal affairs ....."

The crash came three years later. In 1692, "A process having been raised by [Burntisland's] creditors for payment of the debts of the Burgh, some of the Bailies were imprisoned, and the town became bankrupt. It was proposed to assign the whole revenue to the creditors, but the town's Advocate, Mr Monnypenny, advised that some other arrangement should be made. An arrangement was effected accordingly, but in what way, is not recorded. The Bailies, however, were liberated, and the business of the town went on as usual."

There was more financial trouble around 1700, when "A petition was sent to Parliament for a grant of two pennies on the pint of ale used in the Burgh, setting forth that owing to the decay of trade and the loss of shipping during the late war, they were unable to bear the ordinary expenses of the town, or to maintain the works of the harbour." Speed continues: "Owing to the embarrassed state of the town's financial affairs, the requisite number of Councillors could not this year be obtained, and the Burgh was in consequence disfranchised. The collective community managed the revenue with the concurrence of the creditors. The Council was afterwards restored by a poll vote of the burgesses."

Conscription

As well as making a significant contribution to national taxation, each royal burgh had to deliver its share of recruits for the army and navy. As with taxation, the royal burghs of Scotland had an overall target. This total was divided among the individual burghs according to population.

The civil wars and other conflicts of the 17th century are discussed in more detail in Chapter IV. Here we confine ourselves to a brief description of the effect on Burntisland of the Town Council's obligation to supply men for the armed forces.

Speed mentions various occasions on which Burntisland men were selected to serve in the army and navy, and it is likely that there were many more which were unrecorded.

Speed's first record is of Burntisland's having to supply 18 men for the navy around 1624, although he does not say how they were selected. No doubt the Town Council would have tried to find volunteers first, but it is likely that they would also have had to employ a degree of coercion. In the same year, "the Privy Council ordered the Magistrates to provide pilots and seamen to carry His Majesty's ship 'Assurance' to the Thames. The Council reported that there were no pilots of sufficient skill here, and that all the sailors had fled for fear of the press[-gang]."

We do know that there was another massive recruitment exercise in Scotland in 1627. Despite the misgivings of the King, the aim was to raise 14,000 men to fight in the armies of France, Denmark and Sweden in the Thirty Years War. Burntisland would have been expected to supply its share, as it had done on earlier occasions in that war.

Burntisland was also one of the main embarkation ports in 1627, and there was serious disorder in the town as the men gathered to await their ships. A description of those soldiers gives us clues to their previous roles in life - the officers were "men of good family, both Highland and Lowland", but the rank and file were "a riffraff of incorrigible beggars and vagabonds picked up from the highways, [and] criminals released from the gaols". It is only fair to add that, whatever their condition when they embarked, the Scots soldiers in the Thirty Years War gained a remarkable reputation as extremely effective and well disciplined fighting men.

The following extracts from James Speed's notes describe some of the effects on Burntisland of the demand for soldiers to serve in the Scots Army of the Covenant from 1639 to Cromwell's invasion in 1650.

James Speed:
1639, May 7. Volunteers. Twenty five men came voluntarily forward and offered to go with the army to the south. The Council ordained that all those who had gone to the 'Boundred' should be admitted Burgesses free.

..... 1640. Levies. The Council selected fifteen men to go to the south with Colonel Leslie. Others, but it is not said how many, were sent to the north to 'Major Colonel Munro'. Shortly afterwards the 'Council of War of Fife' ordered out every eighth man and another eighth to be in readiness. On the 1st May every fourth man was ordered out, but whether in addition to the former levy does not appear. 'A list of valorous men' was sent to the Committee of the shire at Kirkcaldy. The minister gave a list from the communion roll, but stated that many of these were not 'able men nor of strength for the war'. Every person worth 200 merks was called on to furnish a horse for service. The whole levy is given at forty nine men 'besides boys and horses'. Along with these all 'masterless men, loiterers at home and beggars', were ordered to be sent to the army.

..... 1640. Runaways. All soldiers who had returned from the army were ordered to be apprehended and sent back, and a new levy was ordered in place of those who had not been found.

..... 1640. Cowards. Those men who had been appointed to join the Earl of Dunfermline's regiment and had failed to do so were ordered to be apprehended and stand at the Kirk door with 'rock and spindle' in their hands, and a paper on their heads with an inscription in large letters setting forth their 'infamy' and to be declared enemies to the true religion, and then banished.

..... 1641. Returned Soldiers. Many persons returned from the army this year. These having been ordered to give up their arms, Lord Balgonie sent a letter to the Council 'desiring them not to be so rigourous as to demand Hugh Barclay, trooper, his horse from him, as it was contrary to the law of nations and arms to do so'. The Council thought 'it no way meet to comply with this request, in respect that there is an Act of Parliament commanding all to give up their arms'. It appears, however, that Master Hugh retained his charger, the value of which was said to be 100 merks.

..... c1645. Irish rebels. Sir James Wemyss of Bogie, by authority of the Council of War of Fife, ordered all men belonging to the town between 16 and 60 years of age to be ready fully armed to go to Kinross to oppose the Irish rebels who were within six miles of Perth.

..... In 1645, of 1,879 men appointed to be levied by the Burghs for military service, 16 were assigned to Burntisland; 574 to Edinburgh; to Cupar 24; to Dunfermline 12; Dysart 31; Kinghorn 14; Kirkcaldy 46; St Andrews 30.

Conscription continued in the time of Cromwell's occupation. In 1655, his military commander, Colonel Fairfax, ordered Burntisland Town Council "to apprehend and give up to him all idle men and women between the ages of twenty and forty years, in order to be sent to Barbadoes. Clothes were to be supplied to those in want of them and a groat a day allowed to each till they were received on shipboard. The Council refused to comply till they knew if the gospel were preached at Barbadoes." The outcome of this imaginative stalling tactic is not known.

Subsequent examples of 'recruitment' are -

❖ 1664. 22 Burntisland men required for the navy. No volunteers forthcoming, so the Town Council selected them.
❖ 1689. Six men sent to the navy. They may have been chosen by the drawing of lots.
❖ 1693. Six men recruited for the army, five of whom had to be arrested and imprisoned to secure their compliance.
❖ 1698. Two men required for the army. Chosen by roll of the dice, but both absconded.

View of Burntisland by Andrew Wilson. National Galleries of Scotland.

IV   The Church, the Covenanters and Cromwell

Burntisland's first known church at the Kirkton is described in Chapter I. It survived the Reformation in 1560, apparently escaping unscathed at a time when many church buildings were being desecrated. But within a generation it would be deemed inadequate for its task, and allowed to deteriorate slowly into the picturesque ruin which survives to this day and which is pictured on page 17.

In the period we are looking at, the national Church of Scotland was Roman Catholic prior to the Reformation of 1560. Thereafter it was Protestant - at times episcopalian with bishops, and at other times Presbyterian. Regardless of its form, it was always a powerful institution, exerting great influence on the monarch and parliament, and therefore on national affairs. At a local level, it was responsible, not just for religious matters, but also for education, for looking after the poor, and for punishing the sinners. In the country areas, it would carry out these responsibilities in association with the local landowners. However, in the self governing royal burghs, the church had to work with the town councils. This sometimes created difficulties.

In Burntisland, for example, the Town Council represented only the burgh part of the parish, whereas the church covered the whole parish and was subject to influence from the landowners from outside the burgh. James Speed's notes give us a picture of fairly good relations between the Town Council and the church for most of the time, with a spirit of give and take prevailing when times were hard. The most serious disagreements related to the building of the new Parish Church.

The Burntisland Burgh Charter of 1541 was granted on condition that the Royal Burgh of Burntisland "shall build a good church and shall have caused it to be raised to be a collegiate church of at least six chaplains". Interestingly, the onus here is on the burgh, not the local church.

In any case, the increase in population in the area round the harbour (i.e. within the Royal Burgh) meant that the church at the Kirkton was becoming too small and too remote. And so it was that the burgesses and ordinary folk of the burgh took the decision to press ahead with the construction of the new Parish Church, which began in 1592. Such an undertaking would normally have been financed by the church heritors (the local landowners), but Burntisland's new Parish Church in East Leven Street was very much a community effort, augmented by some financial assistance from other royal burghs.

Although not yet complete, it opened for business in 1594, thirty-four years after the start of the Reformation in Scotland. Needless to say, the Town Council took the view that everyone should worship in the new church. However the heritors (backed by the folk who lived in the landward part of the parish) wanted services to continue at the Kirkton. It would be another 38 years before this dispute was resolved.

James Speed:

1598 ..... The fabric of the New Kirk was completed at this time, a bell put in the steeple, and public worship celebrated there, but the landward heritors refusing to pay their part of the Minister's stipend unless he preached at the Old Kirk at the Kirkton. Mr William Simpson, who had been duly appointed Minister craved leave of the Council to be allowed to officiate there; and further desired them if they would not allow this, to obtain another Minister "that can live on his ain, for there is no remeid for him but to pass to the Auld Kirk or want his stipend". On this representation the Council applied to the King and Privy Council to have the Minister interdicted from preaching at the Auld Kirk, and to compel the landward people to absent themselves from it.

..... For many years after the church had been built and partly furnished, the landward heritors opposed its being constituted the Parish Church, and refused to pay Minister's stipend unless he officiated at the Old Kirk at the Kirkton. After long litigation before the church courts and the Lords Modificators, [the new church] was in 1632 constituted the Parish Church.

James Speed gives a comprehensive description of the new Parish Church building, which is included in Appendix A.

Over the next hundred years, the ministers in the new church would have no easy task - they would have to cope, not only with the effects of their individual eccentricities, but also with the frequent and often unpredictable changes in the national religious climate.

1601 was a significant year for Burntisland. The General Assembly of the Church of Scotland was held in the town. It was there that King James VI first proposed a new translation of the Bible, a proposal which led in due course to the publication of the King James version in 1611.

James Speed:

General Assembly and Council - A meeting of the General Assembly of the Church was held at Burntisland on the 10th March 1601, at which the King was present. The only notice of this meeting in the Council Record is the following:-

"Apud Burntisland tertio Mch. 1601. The Baillies and Council quhais names follow, viz x x x being convenit togidder in counsall ordains an convenient house to be providit for ye convention of ye ministerie with His Majesty and his commissioners to be halden wt-in yee burgh on the tent day of Mch instant and ordains cules to be providit to serve for fyre for ye said house, during the time of the said convention; and all in ane voice thinks Mr Andro Wilson his lodging most convenient for ye purpose and requires him to spare ye same to that effect."

The Mr Andro Wilson referred to was common clerk, and his lodging was at the South Hill. This house would probably be for lodging the members. The meetings of the Assembly would likely be held in the new Kirk.

It has usually been accepted that Speed's assumption was correct, and that the General Assembly was held in the Parish Church. But it has also been suggested that it may have taken place in the house of Andro Wilson, which would have been a substantial dwelling.

The General Assembly of 1601 also took a decision with more direct and immediate implications for local folk - the ratifying of the demotion of the Rev William Watson and his transfer from the high profile charge of St Giles in Edinburgh to Burntisland Parish Church.

And so it was that, later in 1601, William Watson became Minister of Burntisland. He came with a track record of opposition to King James VI, and as a result had already found himself in jail on several occasions.

The year 1606 saw him in trouble again, when he was one of eight Church of Scotland ministers to visit the King in London. The Church of Scotland might have been a reformed church, but James VI was keen to reintroduce bishops. The high powered delegation of Scotland's leading Presbyterian ministers were hoping to persuade James of the error of his ways.

On the right: Burntisland Parish Church from the south. Gavin Anderson.

On the opposite page: Burntisland Parish Church interior. Gavin Anderson.

50

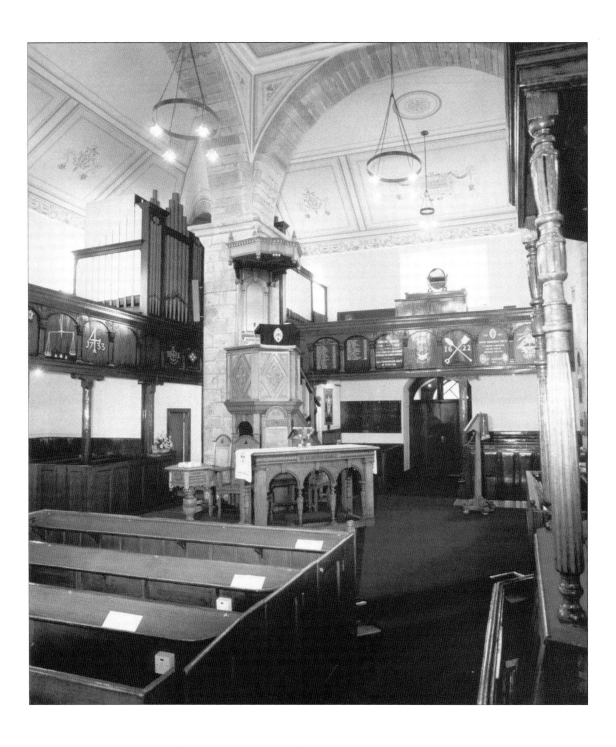

The interior of Burntisland Parish Church, showing the pulpit. On the front of the galleries are some of the old decorative panels which are described in Chapter VII. Gavin Anderson.

The Magistrates' Seat in Burntisland Parish Church. This was originally built for Sir Robert Melville of Rossend Castle in 1606, but was transferred to the Magistrates and Town Council of Burntisland when the Council bought the castle and estate. Gavin Anderson.

The Rev William Watson and Burntisland's 'Amazone weemen' make short work of the Queen's Chamberlain. Pen and ink drawing by Keli Clark.

But they had been tricked, and instead found themselves on trial. Two were never allowed to return to Scotland. The other six, including William Watson of Burntisland, were jailed. They were released after a few months, and allowed to return home - but they were subject to strict conditions, and were not allowed to travel outside their parishes.

William Watson certainly found plenty to occupy himself with locally, and in due course was reckoned to be the most influential person in the town. His language sometimes gave cause for concern, though. In a row with the Town Council, he was alleged to have "used sundry injurious and blasphemous words nought worthy to be repeated".

Watson continued to be a thorn in the flesh of the establishment, and something of a champion of the ordinary folk. When a number of local people were threatened with eviction from their homes in 1615, he led a violent demonstration against the authorities. This was ground breaking behaviour in itself, but so was the fact that the demonstrators were "ane multitude of weemen, above ane hundir, off the bangstar Amazone kind". They confronted the Queen's Chamberlain, who had come to give notice of eviction to the unfortunate tenants, at the Market Cross in the High Street. There the Chamberlain was "maist uncourteously dung off his feet, and his witness with him, they all hurt and bloodit, all his letters and precepts reft frae him, riven and cast away, and sae staned and chased out of the toun". Clearly the women of Burntisland in 1615 were not content to sit at home, knitting socks and making the tea.

This direct action - unprecedented in Scotland - was, unfortunately, the last straw as far as Watson's tenure of Burntisland was concerned. The King decided that he should be moved on again, and in 1616 he was sent to Markinch - with strict instructions that he was never again to come within eight miles of Burntisland.

John Michaelson was appointed Minister of Burntisland in 1616. One of Scotland's most distinguished churchmen, he had nevertheless done a theological U-turn and abandoned his Presbyterian beliefs. He now supported the concept of church government with bishops, which James VI had gradually reintroduced between 1606 and 1612. This immediately placed him at odds with most of his congregation, for Burntisland was a Presbyterian town.

Charles I became King in 1625, and pursued an episcopal agenda. He arranged a separate Scottish Coronation for 1633, and continued to press the case for bishops in the Kirk. On his way home, he lost a fortune which we can still only guess at, when one of the Burntisland ferries which he had chartered sank in a storm. This tragedy is covered in more detail in Chapter VI.

Throughout this period, the Rev Dr Michaelson and his congregation maintained an uneasy truce, but matters were to come to a head in 1638 - the year of the National Covenant.

The signing of the National Covenant on 28 February 1638 in Greyfriars Churchyard was one of the most significant events in the history of Scotland. Scotland had been growing ever more mistrustful of Charles I, in particular his introduction of a new prayer book which was regarded as verging on Roman Catholicism by post-reformation Scottish Presbyterians. Alexander Henderson, Minister of Leuchars, was the prime mover in the drawing up of the National Covenant, which, while careful to acknowledge the authority of the King, reaffirmed the struggle against 'popery'; declared resistance to changes in worship made without the agreement of the people's representatives; and pledged the signatories to defend their religion against all comers.

The nobles signed on 28 February, the ministers and representatives of the burghs on the following day, and then the general population. Within a few weeks it had been signed by representatives of all the counties and all but three of the towns. In Burntisland it was signed "with tearis of great joy". Rarely before or since has Scotland been so united.

James Speed:
The Burgesses of Burntisland were generally zealous covenanters, and scarcely less intolerant in principle than was the faction by which they were often oppressed. Succeeding generations owed much of the religious and civil liberty they enjoyed to the covenanters, in spite of what we now see to have been defect[s] in their protestantism. He must indeed have a cold heart that can look otherwise than with admiration on their zeal, and with sympathy on their sufferings in the cause of what they believed to be truth.

As Speed notes, in the early Covenanting days Burntisland was a stronghold of the movement. However, not only did Dr Michaelson ignore the views of his flock, but he also ignored instructions from the Kirkcaldy Presbytery of the Church of Scotland to subscribe to the Covenant and to read it in church. On five successive Sundays in May and June of 1638, his services were boycotted by the congregation. When the General Assembly of the Church of Scotland, meeting in Glasgow in November 1638, abolished episcopacy and excommunicated the bishops, Dr Michaelson again refused to accept the decision.

The local folk and the Kirkcaldy Presbytery had had enough. Dr Michaelson was found guilty of various charges, and removed from office early in 1639. By then an old man, he continued to live in Burntisland, at his daughter's house in the High Street. He was treated with a fair measure of tolerance in his final years.

His daughter's commemorative marriage lintel was rescued when her old home was demolished, and has been set in the wall of the pend leading from the High Street to Somerville Square - marking the spot where the old house once stood. It has the initials 'RR' for Richard Ross and 'AM' for Agnes Michaelson, and the date 1626.

This whole period was one of great nervousness for Scotland in general and Burntisland in particular. James Speed tells us of the consequences.

James Speed:

1638. During the year 1638 the proceedings of the Council indicated a resolution to resist the government[5] by force. Before this, weapon showings and drillings were held by order of Government; now they were held by order of the Town Council in conjunction with the landward gentlemen of the shire. Drillings were held daily under drill masters sent by the latter. The inhabitants went about their ordinary avocations armed with sword and dagger. Measures were also adapted for fortifying the town.

1639. The nobility and gentry of the shire ordered that the inhabitants be armed and officers appointed; that "Forths and Strongths" be made, at some of which the parishioners of Aberdour were ordered to assist. The West Broom Hill was accordingly fortified and provided with twenty two men.

..... there were earthern and wooden works constructed for the defence of the town along the Broom Hill, and stone batteries at the south side of the Harbour, called "forths", all mounted with great guns.

1640. The Magistrates were at this time constantly occupied about military affairs. The town was enclosed on all sides. Those leaving it were not allowed to return. Ships attempting to land were ordered to be destroyed. Powder and other munitions of war were searched for and put in a place of safety. The tenth penny of the rent of all heritages within the Burgh was exacted. "Three substantious honest men" were appointed to sit for four hours every day to receive contributions of gold and silver work for the public use.

Cromwell's Invasion

In 1643, the notorious witch hunter, John Smith, was appointed Minister of Burntisland. Smith's exploits in tracking down witches struck fear into the women of the town, and these events are covered in Chapter VIII.

By the time of the Rev Smith's appointment, both Scotland and England were engaged in civil war against King Charles I. Initially Cromwell in England had the support of the Scottish Army of the Covenant under General Leslie, and the Rev Smith was called into service as an army padre.

However, the Scots were becoming increasingly nervous about the growing power of Cromwell. In 1647, in a dramatic U-turn, they struck a secret deal with Charles I in which he committed himself to a Presbyterian Britain. Cromwell's execution of the King in 1649 horrified the Scots and accelerated their alienation from Cromwell. They immediately proclaimed Charles II King of Scots.

Seeing the way the wind was blowing in England, Charles II headed north and arrived in Scotland in June 1650. To secure Scottish support, he committed himself to the principles of the National Covenant. He was crowned King of Scots at Scone on New Year's Day, 1651.

---

[5] The 'government' here means the King and his supporters.

Above: Burntisland troops prepare for the arrival of Cromwell. Drawing by Douglas Gray.

Below: Burntisland's Provost fears the worst after Cromwell's army fire their first shot. Pen and ink drawing by Keli Clark.

Meanwhile, Cromwell had invaded Scotland in July 1650 and had made rapid progress. In July 1651 his forces crossed the Forth at Queensferry, routed the Scottish army at Inverkeithing, and advanced on Burntisland. The town's defences had been personally inspected by the King five months before and it was as well prepared as it was ever going to be, with 40 cannon and 500 men ready to defend it. Local folk, both men and women, had laboured long and hard to construct earthen defences.

By 27 July, the enemy had taken up position in the Grange Road area. Facing them were cannon mounted on the East and West Broomhills. It is unlikely these were fired, however, because negotiations between the two sides began immediately. There seems to have been little criticism of the subsequent Burntisland surrender - the town was facing a far superior enemy, the most efficient fighting force in Europe. The surrender saved lives, and left the town intact. The occupation of Burntisland and of Scotland would last for nine years.

In August 1651, the King returned to England, accompanied by a Scots army. Cromwell pursued him and won a convincing victory at Worcester. Charles fled to France in October, and Cromwell's position was secure in both Scotland and England.

James Speed:

1652. Military Rule. There is a blank in the Burgh records from 1646 to 1652. At the latter date the town was in possession of the army of the Commonwealth, and was garrisoned by two and sometimes by three companies of soldiers of about 100 men each, partly horse and partly foot. The town house being occupied by the military, the Burgh Courts were held in a hired house. The community lived under the despotic rule of Colonel Lilburne, the military commander. The Magistrates were subordinate to him, and were employed in little else apparently than raising supplies and providing supplies for his soldiers. No one was allowed to cross the Ferry without a pass from him.

..... 1656. The headquarters of the military force was at this time at the Castle of Burntisland. Captain Roger, the officer in command, sent an imperative order to the Magistrates to send four beds for him and his attendants.

There are three enduring tales relating to Cromwell's occupation. The first is that his soldiers fired the first shot, a cannonball, which hit the Provost's china shop, precipitating instant capitulation. The second is that Burntisland surrendered on condition that Cromwell repaired the harbour and paved the streets. James Speed shows that, whatever may have been promised, Cromwell's sole contribution to these works was a niggardly 33 pounds sterling. The third story is that he stayed in Burntisland on the nights of 29 and 30 July 1651, at the house at 35 High Street (old numbering).

The sad reality about the period of Cromwell's occupation is that it was one of terrible privation and suffering for the local folk, many of whom fled to Aberdour and elsewhere. There is a deep irony in the fact that the Town Council of later years saw fit to name one of the town's principal thoroughfares 'Cromwell Road'.

With the death of Cromwell in 1658 and the increasing unpopularity of Puritan rule throughout Britain, the restoration of the Monarchy became inevitable and Charles II returned from exile in 1660. Initially popular in Scotland, he soon forgot his promises made eleven years before and set about rebuilding an episcopal form of church government. In 1662, Church of Scotland ministers were obliged to subject themselves to examination and approval by a bishop, without which they could no longer continue in office. George Nairne, Minister of Burntisland, had been imprisoned in Edinburgh Castle in 1660 for criticising the King, and was one of some 300 ministers who were banned for refusing to subject themselves to the new ruling.

James Speed:
1662. "The Declaration" acknowledging the King's supremacy in all matters and over all persons, civil and ecclesiastical, was at this time offered for subscription to all persons in office, including the Magistrates, Councillors and other men in office in the Burghs. "The Declaration" was contrary to that principle which rejects the authority of the civil power in matters ecclesiastical; and rather than acknowledge the existence of such, many of all ranks now suffered persecution. By the abuse of his power, the King had brought the established church to the external form of Episcopacy but there was no sincere acquiescence, scarcely indeed the appearance of it, amongst the inhabitants of Burntisland. The reluctance of the Town Councillors to subscribe the "Declaration" appears from their deferring from time to time to do so for what seems very inadequate reasons. Their fear of giving offence to the government appears also from the fact that they never directly or formally refused.

During the 1660s and 1670s, persecution of the dissenting ministers and their congregations increased markedly. It became an offence punishable by death to preach at a conventicle (an open air service taken by a dissenting minister). The Town Council and the ordinary folk of Burntisland were sympathetic to the Covenanters. The council did what it could to avoid implementing the draconian edicts coming from the King. These episcopalian edicts were meekly accepted by the Scottish Parliament, whose capacity for bending in the wind was never more clearly demonstrated.

By the 1670s, the Town Council of Burntisland was reduced to a small rump of pliant burgesses. The majority of burgesses demonstrated their covenanter sympathies by the simple expedient of refusing to take on any council responsibilities.

In 1679, the murder of Archbishop Sharp by a group of Covenanters near St Andrews led to the 'Killing Time' of the 1680s. All Covenanters were hunted down ruthlessly, and summarily executed. One of their leaders, David Hackston from Cupar, was used to provide a grisly reminder to the people of Burntisland that they should toe the line.

Hackston was captured at the Battle of Airds Moss in 1680, taken to Edinburgh naked on horseback, interrogated, condemned, and sentenced as follows: "That his body be drawn backward on a hurdle to the Cross of Edinburgh; that there be a high scaffold erected a little above the Cross, where in the first place his right hand is to be struck off, and after some time his left hand; that he is to be hanged up and cut down alive, his bowels to be taken out, and his heart to be shown by the hangman to the people; then his heart and his bowels to be burned in a fire prepared for that purpose on the scaffold; that afterward his head be cut off, and his body divided into four quarters, his head to be fixed on the Netherbow, one of his quarters with both his hands to be affixed at St. Andrews, another quarter at Glasgow, a third at Leith, a fourth at Burntisland."

Hackston was executed on 30 July 1680. A quarter part of his body was ferried to Burntisland and put on public display at theEast Port, at the east end of the High Street.

The other end of Burntisland High Street was the scene of another distressing event involving Covenanter prisoners in May 1685. A total of 224 men and women were brought to Burntisland by ferry from Leith and imprisoned for two days and two nights in the Tolbooth at the west end of the High Street. The conditions were appalling. The prisoners were packed into the very restricted space, and denied food and water. John Blyth commented: "Had the weather been hot, these two 'strait' rooms in Burntisland Tolbooth might easily have set a precedent for the Black Hole of Calcutta."

While incarcerated in Burntisland Tolbooth, the prisoners were asked to swear an oath of allegiance, acknowledging the King's supremacy over religious opinions. A handful agreed. The remainder, including the old, infirm and pregnant, and with their hands tied behind their backs, were escorted from Burntisland through the East Port, on the first stage of a forced march to Dunnottar Castle near Stonehaven. They were imprisoned there in equally deplorable conditions. The remote location had been chosen because of an anticipated rescue attempt. Three months later, when the prospect of rescue had receded, the survivors were marched back to Burntisland and ferried to Leith. Most were banished, as slave labour, to the American plantations, and many died on that final journey.

At Stenhouse, about two miles to the north west of Burntisland, are the ruins of a two-storey 17th century house called Knockdavie. It was the home of Colonel John Douglas, a close ally of John Graham of Claverhouse ('Bluidy Clavers' or 'Bonnie Dundee', depending on your point of view). Douglas served with Graham in the ruthless hunting down of Covenanters in the Killing Time. The King rewarded Douglas by appointing him Secretary of War for the armed forces in Scotland. The Covenanters, however, added his name to their 'Black List of Persecutors' as a murderer, harasser and spoiler. There was a satisfactory end to the story for the Covenanters, who recorded that "his wicked honours were short lived; his name soon became extinct, having neither root nor branch, male nor female, for a remembrance of him."

In 1685, James VII succeeded his father as King. But the Stewarts' days were numbered. In November 1688, William, Prince of Orange, landed at Torbay, and James VII fled in December. The Killing Time ended, and Presbyterianism was secure. On 8 January 1689, the Declaration of the Prince of Orange was read at the Market Cross, Burntisland.

Given their Presbyterian beliefs, most of the citizens of Burntisland would have welcomed the accession of William and Mary. But it was to usher in another era of persecution, although this time it was the episcopalians who were to suffer. James Speed tells us how Burntisland treated James Inglis, a minister with unsound episcopalian tendencies.

James Speed:
1693. Mr James Inglis from St Martin's, had been presented to be minister of the parish ..... The Council opposed his admission before the Presbytery of Dunfermline, on what grounds is not stated. The objections of the Council were repelled by the Presbytery, and, with the concurrence of the landward heritors, the case was carried to the superior court. ..... Mr Inglis was admitted on the 14th August; but the Council refused to acknowledge him as minister, and took possession of the boxes used for collecting money for the poor, and of the kirk session records.

In 1699, by desire of the council and the landward heritors, the Presbytery held a visitation of the parish, which resulted in Mr Inglis being formally accused of preaching erroneous doctrine, and of negligence in the discharge of his duty. After a long trial, he was suspended from the functions of the ministry sine die, and the parish declared vacant. This Mr Inglis had at first received episcopal ordination, or, as it was expressed, had been ordained by the curates. He dispensed the communion only once during his incumbency.

Unsoundness of doctrine was not the only failing to afflict Burntisland's ministers. James Pitcairn, Minister from 1688 to 1691, fell from grace following an unseemly brawl with a Kirkcaldy miller in a field between Burntisland and Kinghorn. It appears that the Rev Pitcairn gained inspiration by relaxing in local fields, accompanied by his large dog. In April 1689, John Williamson, a Kirkcaldy miller, was on his way home from Burntisland with his wife, who was on horseback. The minister's dog attacked the horse, throwing the unfortunate Mrs Williamson to the ground. The resulting fisticuffs between Pitcairn and Williamson kept the local courts busy for some time.

Stipends and Manses

There was often a struggle to raise the money required to pay the town's minister. And there were occasions when he received no payment at all. But usually the Town Council came to the rescue and made up any shortfall, as James Speed explains.

<u>James Speed:</u>
To supplement the Minister's stipend the Burgh contributed sums varying from 200 to 400 merks yearly. It settled down at the latter sum, at which it still remains. This was originally raised by assessment on the inhabitants, along with the other taxes for national and local purposes. But during the civil wars of the seventeenth century, it being found impossible to levy the whole of the taxes demanded from the inhabitants for these purposes, the corporate revenue was drawn on to make up the deficiency of the Minister's and Schoolmaster's stipends. In this manner these payments glided into permanent charges on the Burgh revenue.

Up to 1656, the town's minister lived in the old manse at the Kirkton, close to the original church. It is marked on the map on page 14, described as the 'Old Manse in Ruins'. Its foundations now lie forgotten, on the east side of what is now Church Street.

In 1656, the old manse was deemed inadequate and "the Minister received £20 from the town and £40 from the heritors, in place of a Manse. This agreement was continued till a late period."

So the minister would have had to find his own accommodation; and perhaps even build his own home. There is evidence that the ministers lived in a house in what we now call Forth Place, on the site of the new flats opposite the main dock gates. There would have been a garden stretching south to the seashore. Forth Place was quite different in those days, before the railway and the East Dock, and with the sea lapping at the rocks close to where the dock gates now stand.

We do know that, in the early 19th century, the Rev James Wemyss sold 'the manse in Forth Place' to the church, and that a new manse was built there in 1824. Around 1845, it was sold to the railway company and became the Forth Hotel. A replacement manse was erected in Cromwell Road, and it survives as Grayforth House Nursing Home.

On the next two pages: J. Wood's plan of Burntisland, dated 1824. Several versions of this plan exist, although the differences are small. The plans were produced as evidence in a legal dispute, and each interested party had his or her own customised copy. The surviving copies are all of poor quality, making them difficult to read. But the plan does give a good idea of how Burntisland looked at a time when there was still a tolbooth at the west end of the High Street. National Library of Scotland.

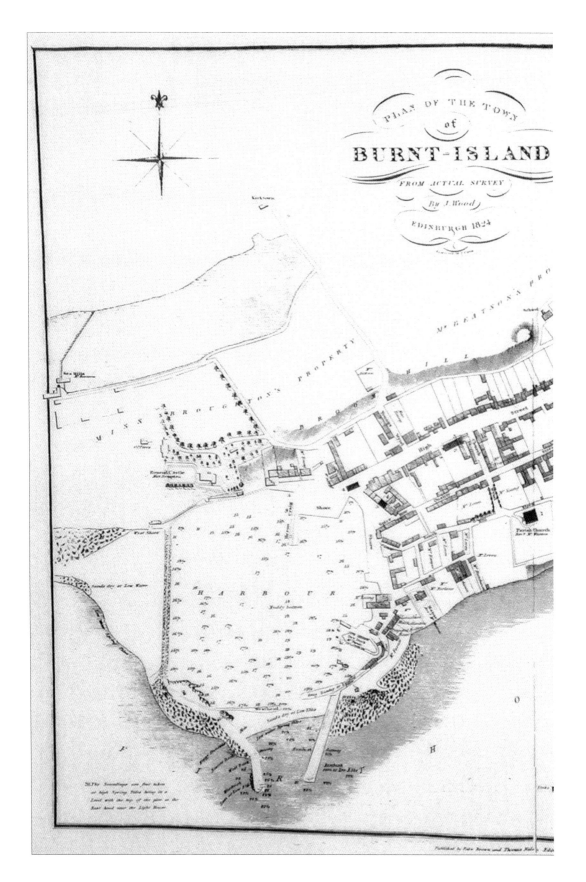

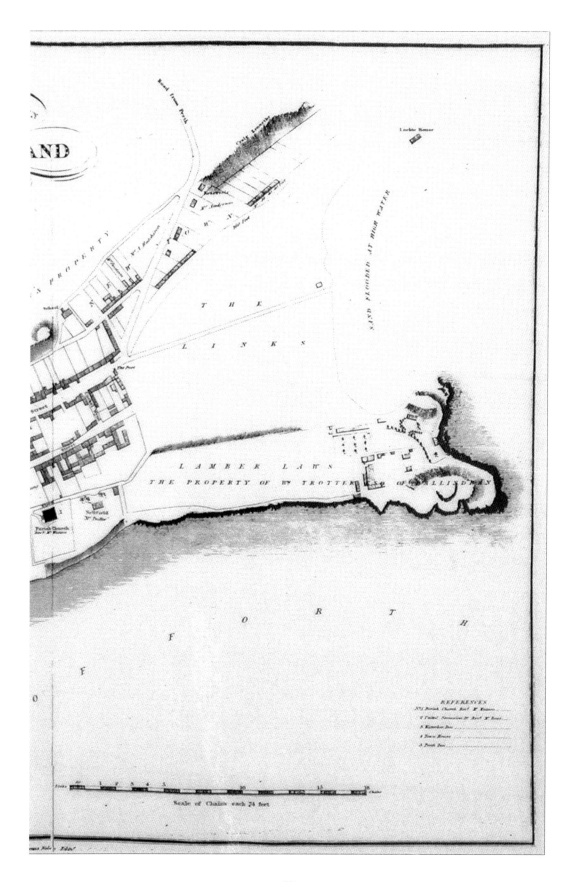

V   The Town: its Buildings and People

There has been a settlement at the Kirkton from at least the 12th century. The concept of the town of Burntisland was unknown then, although there may well have been a number of fishermen living in what is now the harbour area.

The harbour itself took on much greater significance when it was realised what an asset it could become if it was developed to take ships of the Scottish navy. It is likely that the number of folk living close to the harbour was beginning to expand in the 15th century. It is equally likely that they would see themselves as Burntisland folk and distinct from the inhabitants of the Kirkton village.

John Slezer's late 17th century drawing of the town (reproduced on the inside front cover) shws that by then there were a large number of substantial buildings around the harbour. They appear to be built of stone, like the Parish Church which also features in the drawing.

James Speed:
Streets. At the end of the sixteenth century houses had been built along the east side of the Harbour and in a continuous line on both sides of the King's High Street as far as the East Port. Parallel to this street was the Back Gate on the south, but the houses do not seem to have been continuous. Farther south was the South Hill having detached houses with gardens. The Kirk Wynd is referred to, and the North Vennel leading to the Kirkton. There were also narrow lanes passing between some of the streets called "Throughs". Between the north side of the High Street and the Broom Hill were gardens, malt kilns, and brew houses. In the middle of the seventeenth century the High Street was partly paved, with a gutter on each side, and the Back Street, with a gutter in the middle. These works had been very imperfectly executed, and were not completed till the end of that century. The gutters were partly of wood. From the frequent orders issued to clear the streets of red and middings, and to make trenches to allow the water to run off, it may be inferred that the streets were in a very bad condition.

Port. At the east end of the High Street an arch was built across the street in 1635, and called the East Port. It was taken down in 1825[6] by order of the Road Trustees, for the purpose of widening the entrance. Though this erection had no pretensions to architectural beauty, it gave the town a venerable appearance to those entering it from the east, and formed a shelter from the easterly winds. The Trustees promised to erect a handsome structure in place of it. The two square pillars built there shew what was these gentlemen's idea of handsomeness. The South Port and the North Port are referred to in the record, but at what particular point these were I have not discovered. If there were any buildings connected with them, they have long since disappeared.[7]

..... Till about the middle of the last century[8] the communication with the county was by roads fit to be used by persons travelling on foot or on horseback. The required width was no more than sufficient to allow two horses carrying creels to pass each other. The road to the north passed by the Kirkton, Grange and Dunearn to Kinross; to the west in front of Geds Mill by where Colinswell house now stands to Aberdour; to the east, through the Links, Lochies and

---

[6] The East Port was almost certainly removed in 1843.
[7] A Coronation menu card from 1902 states that the East Port and the North Port were both built in 1635. It is difficult to envisage the North Port being anywhere other than on the road from Burntisland to the Kirkton, between the West and East Broomhills.
[8] The 18th century.

Bents by the defile at the east end of these, by Kinghorn Loch to Kirkcaldy. These lines of road have been several times altered within the last hundred years.

Although the earliest map of Burntisland which we have is from 1746 (see page 32), the layout of streets shown there would have been in existence for many years before. The first houses were concentrated around the harbour, and the town gradually spread eastwards. The town's hub became the King's High Street and the Shore (which is now, broadly speaking, Harbour Place and Seaforth Place). The merchants would have had their premises in the High Street, and the shipmasters would be living in substantial dwellings at the Shore, where they could keep a close eye on shipping movements.

The professional classes, some of whom also had homes in Edinburgh, built their houses in Quality Street (now Somerville Square) and at the South Hill (in the area now occupied by West Leven Street and South Hill Street). This latter area has changed considerably of course, as a result of the railway developments of the 1840s and 1880s, but we can get an idea of what it looked like in early times from Humble's painting on page 28.

The Charters, Fairfax, Wemyss and Leven families all lived in this area. They traded properties between themselves as well as intermarrying. All of them had a good sprinkling of clergymen in their family trees; in fact, the Charters could claim a direct line to John Knox. Mary Somerville, the renowned author and scientist, was the product of a Fairfax/Charters marriage and records in her memoirs that she spent many hours in her garden which ran all the way from Quality Street to the sea.

The attractions of the area were that it was close to both the town centre and the seashore, and very handy for the Granton ferry. These well-to-do families usually had properties in Edinburgh's New Town, as well as in Burntisland, and the ferry link was important to them. However, they do all seem to have looked on Burntisland as their main base.

The working classes would fit in wherever they could find accommodation - many of them in the High Street and its closes and vennels, but predominantly in the teeming warrens of Back Street (now Somerville Street).

Rossend Castle and the two Parish Churches are Burntisland's oldest and finest buildings. A great deal more could be made of the ruins of the old church at the Kirkton, which has not received the care, protection and attention which it merits. On the other hand, the castle and the new parish church are well looked after - although understandably they are not always accessible, because both are working buildings.

Rossend Castle had a narrow escape in 1970, when Burntisland Town Council sent in the bulldozers. But last minute efforts to save the building were successful, and it was bought in 1975 by a firm of architects. It was then imaginatively restored and became the firm's head office.

The preserved group of six domestic buildings on the south side of Somerville Square (formerly, at various times, the Midgait, Quality Street, Back Street and Somerville Street) contains two dating from the late 16th century, although both were modernised in the 1950s. One of them was the home of the Fairfax family; their daughter, later Mary Somerville, grew up there. Despite the changes over the years, this group of buildings gives us a good idea of the types of houses in which Burntisland's leading citizens lived many years ago.

Other town buildings which date from early times are the Star Tavern in the High Street (built in 1671 as a house, and completely rebuilt internally in 1975); and the building at 1-3 Harbour Place, although the current structure is largely a replica with some of the original 16th century features incorporated.

Above: Somerville Street (now Somerville Square) by Andrew Young,
in Burntisland Burgh Chambers. Ian Archibald.

Below: Somerville Square, showing the group of six preserved domestic buildings.
Mary Somerville's house is second from the left (with the tall chimney). Iain Sommerville.

When Mary Somerville's house was being renovated in the 1950s, a number of previously unknown features, including a secret staircase, were revealed. Of much greater historic importance, however, was the discovery of the remains of two very old painted ceilings. Experts were summoned and, after everything had been fully documented and photographed, the ceilings were dismantled and taken to Edinburgh. They are currently in storage at the Stenhouse Conservation Centre in the city.

The ceilings date from the late 16th or early 17th century. They were painted using what is called the 'tempera' technique, which involved the mixing of ground pigments with glue size. One of the two ceilings is known as the astral ceiling, and a reconstruction of it is pictured above. The Sibyl (ancient mythological prophetess) in the photograph on the left is from the second ceiling.

Stenhouse Conservation Centre.

On the opposite page and above: three impressions of old Burntisland
by Anna Crawford Briggs. MacKenzie McGill Galleries.

*Left: the Star Tavern,
built as a house in 1671,
and rebuilt internally in 1975.
Iain Sommerville.*

*Below: Harbour Place.
The building on the left is largely
a replica of a much older one on the
same site, with some of the original
16th century features incorporated.
Iain Sommerville.*

The High Street and East Port, complete with assorted animals and a few middens.
Pen and ink drawing by Keli Clark.

Sadly, there are no surviving working class homes from those days. However, if you were to examine the town from a low flying helicopter, you would be able to identify a fair number of parts of old buildings which are now relegated to secondary uses, and some of which are hidden from normal view by modern structures.

To our eyes, much of the town in the 17th century would have presented an uncomfortable spectacle. With middens everywhere, it would have had a rich aroma. In 1609, an attempt was made to have pigs confined to quarters, rather than roaming the streets. Householders were encouraged to transport their rubbish to reserved areas on the Links, but did so only infrequently if at all. As late as 1781, the Town Council received a petition from the inhabitants, complaining that it was dangerous to walk the streets at night lest they "tumble into ye muck middings and dung hills, or break their heads on ye carts in ye High Street." You might have been relatively safe from muggers, but beggars would accost you at every corner. They were officially discouraged, but some had no other means of support, and therefore no option but to beg. There would also be buskers with bagpipes or the stringed viol, seeking recompense for their efforts while trying to avoid expulsion from the town. In 1631, the church made it an offence to give money to "vagabond, strong, masterful, and bold beggars, and such as call themselves Egyptians". This was an attempt to get rid of the 'professional' beggars.

Lost forever .....

In the three decades following the Second World War, urgent remedial action was taken to replace much of Scotland's older housing stock, which was said to be the worst in Western Europe. It is perhaps understandable that old houses which would now be restored were torn down throughout the country, including Burntisland. Five of the photographs shown here are of buildings which were demolished at that time, and which dated from as early as the 17th century.

On the opposite page: (top) Somerville Street (now Square), north side; (bottom) High Street west, south side. Crown Copyright RCAHMS.

Above: (top right) Kirkgate, east side; (bottom left) High Street/Lothian Street corner; (bottom right) Leven Street. It is believed that Admiral Sir Andrew Wood (c1455-1539), 'Scotland's Nelson', had a home on the site of the High Street/Lothian Street building. Crown Copyright RCAHMS.

The sixth photo is top left on this page: the Old Ship Tavern behind Harbour Place, which was replaced many years earlier. From a picture by Andrew Young.

Population

James Speed:
From the year 1600 and probably before, till near the end of last century[9], the number of the inhabitants seemed to vary very little. In that year and till the time I have stated, there were about 250 names on the stent roll. These were all either heritors or house holders. Allowing 50 more for those unable to pay any direct tax, this would give about 1,200 as the number of the inhabitants.

John Blyth hazarded a guess at the town's population in 1645, and came up with the figure of 960. A more accurate estimate for the year 1755 gave the population of the whole of the parish as 1,390.

In the 1790s, the Rev James Wemyss[10] estimated the population of the Parish of Burntisland at 1,210. He pointed out that this figure represented a decrease on the 1755 estimate, and attributed that to a reduction in shipping activity and changes in farming practices.

By 1801, the population of the parish had grown to 1,530; to 2,136 by 1821; to 2,399 by 1831; and to 3,158 by 1851. (The 1831 parish figure of 2,399 comprised 1,873 in Burntisland town, 190 in the Kirkton village, and 336 in the country areas.)

Rapid expansion continued throughout the rest of the 19th century, fuelled by coal exports and railway and ferry developments. At the time of writing, Burntisland's population is around 6,000, and has been largely unchanged for many years.

Care of the Poor

According to Speed, the number of poor folk requiring assistance from the burgh around 1700 was usually about twenty, most of them women. They were paid from two to four shillings Scots a week. The Town Council rented a house to provide lodgings for the homeless. However, the church was the main provider of support for the poor. Both regular and special collections were made to raise the funds. The Town Council was always keen to be involved in the distribution of the money, and the magistrates usually attended the Kirk Session meetings when this subject was being discussed. Most of the recipients were local folk who had fallen on hard times. Occasionally there were more unusual deserving cases, such as "twelve shillings to Alexander Keith, surgeon in a ship, having his thigh and hips shot through with a cannon ball".

As the guilds and craft associations (discussed in Chapter VII) developed, they took on responsibility for looking after those of their members who were no longer able to earn a living. They also supported the widows and orphaned children of members. The funds for these activities came from members' subscriptions, and provided what were effectively early forms of health and life insurance.

The Watson's Mortification charity was set up in 1693. The benefactor was Captain John Watson, whose business activities were the raising of recruits for the armies of Denmark and Sweden, and the export of horses to these and other countries in northern Europe. He was also a Burntisland Councillor and Magistrate. He left his substantial house in the Midgait (also known as Quality Street, and now Somerville Square) to be divided into three dwellings, for the use of three indigent widows. He also bought land to the north east of the town, to provide an income

---

[9] The 18th century.
[10] In his contribution to the Statistical Account of Scotland, 1791-99.

The Watson headstone in the Parish Churchyard.

for the widows, and in addition fund the school education of poor children from Burntisland. The house is one of the preserved group in Somerville Square, referred to above, and the land donated by Watson is still known locally as the "Widows' Land". Speed commented that the 'hospital' had afforded a comfortable asylum for a succession of poor widows.

Education

The Reformation in Scotland had significant implications for Scottish education. In 1560, John Knox called for a school in every parish. Significant progress was made between then and the end of the 17th century, but the achievements varied considerably from one area to another. Nevertheless, sufficient advances were made for Scotland to gain a fine reputation throughout Europe for the quality of its education. In 1696, the Scottish Parliament passed legislation which provided the legal basis for the fulfilment of Knox's dream - the establishment of the first national education system in the world, reputedly since the days of ancient Sparta. The foundations were well and truly laid for the Scottish Enlightenment of later years.

In the 17th century, in most of Scotland, it was the responsibility of the national church to provide basic schooling. However, in the royal burghs, that task was entrusted to the town councils - although the church was closely involved too.

James Speed:
1596. The records of the Burgh begin this year. ..... There was a reader of public prayers who was also Schoolmaster, but for whom there was no settled provision. For his support, the Council nominated certain of the "honestest men" of the town to lodge him in their houses by turns.

..... 1598. The Council declared that no person shall be allowed to set up a school without their leave.

..... A Schoolmaster and School Doctor[11] were regularly appointed this year; the latter was to be "taker up of the psalm, keeper of the Kirk records, and reader of prayers in the Kirk".

..... In 1612, the Presbytery, in compliance with an ordinance of the Archbishop of St Andrews, ordered the Council to establish a Grammar School within the Burgh. The Council set forth that they "think it not meet to comply therewith", but resolve to have an ordinary School, and to look out for a fit person to be master. It appears that the then incumbent[12] was not considered fit. They afterwards, however, found that as he taught "Inglis" that he was fit, and rented a school house for his accommodation. .....

On this occasion was introduced a custom, continued for many years, of the Master and Doctor delivering the keys of the school-house and of their dwelling houses to the Council in acknowledgement that they held their offices during the pleasure of the Council.

---

[11] Assistant schoolmaster.
[12] David Adamson.

The keys were regularly returned with an admonition to be "more diligent than heretofore". No private schools were allowed except those of women, and they were allowed to teach "lasses and very young boys".

..... In the year 1620, a regular and qualified schoolmaster was appointed with a salary of 100 merks, 50 of which were paid by the Kirk Session, and 50 by the Prime [Gilt]. Twelve shillings were paid quarterly by each scholar, of which two thirds were for the Master and one third for the Doctor. ..... [A] house for a school house [was] rented at eight pounds yearly.

[Also] in 1620, six roods of land were bought at the South Hill, whereon a school-house and dwelling houses for the Master and Doctor were erected. ..... The expense of the mason work is given at sixty six pounds and £34-13-4 for wright work. ..... The place near which they stood still goes under the name of the "Scholars' Brae".

..... 1623. ..... [The] Minister's and Schoolmaster's stipends were raised by an assessment on the inhabitants, and so continued for upwards of 50 years; but afterwards they were paid from the common revenue of the Burgh.

..... In 1635 the salary of the Schoolmaster was 100 merks, afterwards increased to 150. The quarterly fees were, for Latin 12 shillings, for English 9 shillings, of which two thirds belonged to the Master and one third to the Doctor. I see no mention of a salary to the Doctor, but he was usually reader of prayers and precentor in the church, for which he had an allowance.

..... In 1656 a woman teacher had a free house, and in 1743 two pounds sterling were given on condition that she taught two or three scholars free.

In 1803 the old school house was taken down, and a new building erected at the east end of the Broom Hill for school and Master's houses, a shapeless erection, but well aired.[13]

Being the Burntisland schoolmaster in the 17th century was not an easy task. In 1630, the incumbent had an unusual problem with the conduct of his assistant. Speed recorded the episode: "Mr Thomas Christie, Schoolmaster, complained to the Council that the School Doctor went from house to house with his scholars, playing at 'carts' till 12 o'clock at night. The Council advised them to 'patch up the matter, shake hands and drink together' - all which was presently done."

In 1658, the assistant schoolmaster was dismissed "because he could not teach arithmetic nor the rudiments of grammar, and from being Session Clerk because he was 'unfit' ".

A Yorkshireman on a tour of Scotland in 1677 paid a visit to Burntisland school and recorded his impressions of a very basic institution: "We saw the school wherein were two seats for the two masters; the rest were strewed with grass, moss, etc., and all the boys lay there in the litter like pigs in a sty."

The Town Council had no qualms about getting rid of unsuitable teachers. In 1674, the schoolmaster, Francis Hannay, was dismissed following his "inhumane belting of the children". In 1686, the Town Council was asked to intervene in a row between Samuel Ranken, the schoolmaster, and David Christie, his assistant. Christie had used "base and scurvie language" against the master, and had called him a knave and a rascal. The council decided he had been provoked, and gave both men a warning. However, Ranken went too far the following year, when further unacceptable conduct led to his dismissal.

Sometimes there was no money to pay the teachers, When the town was in serious financial difficulties in 1700, "The Burgh School was declared vacant by the Council, because they had not funds to pay the stipends of the Master and Doctor; on which both offered to serve without stipend till Martinmas."

---

[13] This building became the Episcopal School after 1876, when the new burgh school in Ferguson Place opened. It was demolished in the early 1970s.

As Speed notes, fees were charged for education at Burntisland school, and indeed throughout Scotland. It was not until 1890 that primary education was provided free of charge. But there was usually some help available for poor families. For example, in 1684, Burntisland Town Council allocated the income from specified rented lands for the purpose of teaching poor children.

The Plague Epidemics

Being a port, Burntisland was vulnerable to the frequent plague epidemics of the 16th and 17th centuries. However, at the first hint of trouble, the authorities immediately closed the ports on the Fife coast, and this prompt action certainly helped to control the spread of the disease.

Nevertheless, there were outbreaks of plague recorded in Burntisland in 1574 and again in 1602, although we do not know how serious they were. Here James Speed records the precautions which were taken in Burntisland in 1602.

James Speed:

The town was strictly watched day and night, to prevent persons from [infected] places from entering it. Many of the inhabitants were suspected of being infected and therefore 'enclosed' - that is, shut up in their houses. When this was resorted to they were not allowed to come out again without leave from the Council. Inspectors were appointed to examine the suspected, and on their report depended the treatment they experienced. The breaking out of boils on the body was considered a symptom of the disease. As soon as a suspicion of its approach arose, all dogs, cats and swine were ordered to be killed, in the belief apparently that these animals propagated the infection. The streets were ordered to be cleared of 'Middings, red and refuse', and paved gutters were ordered to be made to carry off the standing water. At this time, recruits for the King of Sweden were lodged in the town preparatory to embarkation. These, with all poor persons and beggars, were ordered to be expelled. The inhabitants continued for several years after this to live in a constant state of alarm about the plague. Much of the time of the council seemed to be occupied in making regulations for protection against the infection.

Sadly, there was a further - and much more serious - outbreak in 1608, which Speed described in some detail, as follows.

James Speed:

1608. In spite, however, of all their precautions, the town had a severe visitation of the disease in 1608. On the 27th August, it having been discovered that three or four persons had died of the 'sickness', the Council ordered that 'cleangers' be sought for from Kinghorn to 'tack order with this sickness', and to bury those who had died of it. The Council ordered that the inhabitants were not to hold intercourse with each other. Twenty pounds were paid to the workmen for graves. Two loads of white bread were received as a gift from the inhabitants of Kirkcaldy, for the poor; and thirty pounds were taken from 'the Tuesdays box' for their support. Poor persons, when attacked, were taken from their own houses to 'lodges' on the south side of the Links. If they appeared to be recovering, they were removed to lodges on the north side, and there remained till free from the disease. But nothing belonging to them was permitted to be brought into the town. Some kind of kilns were built and cauldrons for cleansing the 'foul gear' were provided. The cleansers were a disorderly set. They extracted four pounds from the friends of deceased persons for attendance, above the regular allowance, and also abstracted goods in place of money.

An agreement was therefore made with them that they were to have one hundred pounds and their maintenance, till the town was cleansed. It appears that the Magistrates lost almost all authority during this visitation. Crimes and offences of various kinds prevailed to an unusual extent. As some remedy for this state of matters, fourteen persons were appointed with the power of Bailies, and twenty eight assessors. These were ordered to call out the inhabitants to watch by turns.

None were allowed to leave the town lest this duty should be evaded; nor were any allowed to enter it without leave, I presume. The town was in a state of siege, all the neighbouring places having interdicted intercourse with it. On the 28th November the town was considered free from the disease; and those who lodged in the Links were allowed to come in, but not to go at large till trial was made of the state of their health. The 'cleangers' were conveyed to Kinghorn and delivered to the authorities there at the 'West Port thereof'. I have nowhere seen it recorded how many died on this occasion, but it must have been considerable - chiefly poor persons.

Left: nailing in the plague suspects. Drawing by Douglas Gray.

Above: those infected with the plague are taken to the lodges on the Links. Pen and ink drawing by Keli Clark.

There is no record of where Burntisland's plague victims were buried. Practices elsewhere varied, although specially dug mass graves were normally used. These might be in or close to the normal burying ground, or in a more remote location.

In Burntisland in 1608, people would normally be interred in the old Kirkton Churchyard or in the new Churchyard in East Leven Street. It is possible that plague victims were buried at one or both of these locations. Another possibility is the Lammerlaws, where a significant quantity of human remains have been found - although these may have included criminals who had been hung on Gallows Hill or witches who had been burned.

John Blyth provided this evocative description of the burial of plague victims: "The bailies, in gowns of grey, bearing a St. Andrew's Cross before and behind, superintended all measures taken in connection with the disease. The dead were conveyed to the burying ground in close biers covered with black cloth which bore a white cross. Burials took place at night, thereby surely adding an additional touch of dread as, though survivors did not actually see what was taking place, they must have heard the discordant warning bell which hung clanging from the side of each bier."

Although a further outbreak of the plague in 1642 does not appear to have affected Burntisland, the town's good fortune was unlikely to have resulted from an interesting new restriction imposed in that year and recorded by Speed: "A Shipmaster desired to be allowed to land his wife and family, they 'all being by the blessing of God, in good health'. The Council ordered them to remain on board till the full moon." Lunar intervention, indeed.

Not only did Burntisland escape the plague in 1642, but it also got an additional bonus when the Convention of Royal Burghs selected it as the venue for a meeting of the Convention which would normally have been held in Edinburgh. Edinburgh had not been so lucky, and was badly affected by the epidemic of that year.

Protection of the Burgh

We have seen in Chapter III that the Town Council had responsibilities for helping with the defence of the realm, but they also had to arrange for the town itself to be protected and defended.

The most basic task was what was known as 'watching and warding' - men were posted at key points on the burgh's perimeter, to keep an eye open for undesirables of all kinds and prevent them from entering the town. A respectable royal burgh like Burntisland would certainly

Burntisland's militiamen, armed and ready to defend the town. On the left, a pikeman; on the right, a musketeer. Drawings by Douglas Gray.

not want to entertain beggars, vagrants, persons carrying diseases, or dustifoots (a term which encompassed travelling merchants, pedlars and vagabonds). The Town Council had powers to order able-bodied men to carry out these duties.

The town also maintained its own defence force - a sort of Home Guard. Again, the Town Council had wide ranging powers to force men to participate. Here are some examples quoted by James Speed -

❖ 1598. "The inhabitants of the town [were] ordered to provide themselves either with corslet, head piece, sword and pike; or with a musket, staff, head piece and sword."

❖ 1624. "Each Burgess was ordered by the Town Council to provide himself with weapons according to his estate. Such of the inhabitants fit to bear arms were afterwards embodied under the name of militia. There were two companies, one of married and one of unmarried men. Each had a stand of colours with an ensign to carry them; a commander and sergeants 'to keep the men in the ranks at the weapon shawings'."

❖ 1666. "Each person was ordered to declare what arms he possessed, and to repair to the Kirk Wynd with them. Arms were ordered to be provided for those who had none. There were 205 men enrolled as volunteers, of whom 42 were equipped at the town's expense. Of these, two thirds were musqueteers and bandiliers, and one third armed with picks only."

❖ 1667. "The town was attacked by a Dutch Squadron, but it does not appear that much damage was done. The Council appealed to the Lord Commissioner for arms to repel any fresh attack. Some great guns, with suitable ammunition, were sent. All fencible men were ordered to be armed; and some who had fled from the town during the attack were ordered to be punished."

❖ 1688. "The whole fencible men were ordered to meet in the Links in their best array."

VI   Maritime Matters

James Speed:
From the earliest records it appears that the principal inhabitants were seafaring people, navigating their own vessels in foreign and coasting voyages. In 1640 there were nine vessels belonging to the town of 50 tons burthen and upwards, namely one of 50 tons, one of 80 tons, one of 85 tons, one of 105 tons, two of 115 tons, one of 120 tons and one of 160 tons. Besides these there were smaller vessels called crears, employed as coasters. There were also ferry boats, of which some were decked and some open boats, but the exact number I have not seen stated. The providing of accommodation for travellers by the Ferry to and from Leith gave employment to many persons, almost every house appeared to be a regular or occasional place of lodging for travellers. Many were employed in navigating the Ferry Boats, and many in providing horses for travellers. These horses were accompanied on their journeys by men on foot.

Burntisland's fine natural harbour was for centuries the town's principal asset. Leaders as diverse as the Roman governor Agricola, Oliver Cromwell, and the Kings and Queens of Scotland and Great Britain are reputed to have sung its praises and made full use of it.

The harbour's national significance, and the need to safeguard and develop it, were the main factors in the granting of royal burgh status to Burntisland. King James V was the first to capitalise on this unique asset, and it was he who set in train the early development of the modern town. For a year or two prior to his granting of the royal charter of 1541, he had spent significant sums on the building of piers. He also encouraged the development of shipbuilding and the use of the harbour as a naval base. Burntisland soon became second only to Leith in its importance as a seaport on the Firth of Forth.

The harbour had a major strategic role in the nation's defence; it handled a significant amount of trade between Scotland and the rest of Europe; and, as a ferry terminal, it provided the main gateway for travel between the nation's capital, Edinburgh, and much of the country. It also ensured that Burntisland had a national significance much greater than one would expect of such a small town.

James Speed:
About the year 1600 the Harbour appears to have been a slip at the south east corner of the Harbour called the Grey Sunday, for the use of the ferry boats; a pier, or bulwark as it was called, at the north west corner near what is now called the Half Moon, constructed wholly or mostly of wood, and adapted for the reception of the larger class of ships; some kind of work at the Earne Craig (not Iron Craig nor Herring Craig, as it is sometimes called), and probably other piers along the shore.
..... The causeway joining the island to the shore was made in the year 16 [14]. The east head was built about 1620. It was made parallel to the Grey Sunday, apparently for the purpose of sheltering the landing place from the south east wind. The West Head was finished in 1656. These were the only considerable improvements effected on the Harbour works for 150 years after.

---

[14] The year was omitted, but is likely to have been in the period 1600 to 1620.

They were very imperfectly executed, and stood in constant need of repair, forming - as the Council expressed it in their application to the Government and the Conventions for assistance - "an intolerable burden on the town".

As Speed notes, the maintenance of an important harbour like that of Burntisland was always going to be an expensive business. Given its national significance, Burntisland Town Council was able to apply - successfully - for financial assistance for harbour works from the Privy Council and the Convention of Royal Burghs. Here are some examples quoted by Speed -

- ❖ 1642. "The Convention ..... granted 600 merks for repairs on the harbour."
- ❖ 1664. "The works at the harbour were still incomplete, and a warrant was obtained from the Privy Council for a voluntary contribution through the Burghs to assist in repairing and extending them. The following was the result:- Edinburgh gave 280 libs, Aberdeen 186 libs, Leith 41 libs, Arbroath 20 libs, Cannongate 33 libs 6 shillings, Anstruther 29 libs, Glasgow 120 libs, Kilrenny 13 libs 16 shillings, Anstruther Wester 6 libs, Pittenweem 20 libs, Crail 29 libs."
- ❖ 1669. "Application was made to the Convention for a grant of money to be expended on the works connected with the harbour, the maintaining of which being, as the Council sets forth, 'a burden almost intolerable'."
- ❖ 1682. "A general collection was authorised this year by the Privy Council, for repairing the harbour of Burntisland 'which is of such general and great importance'; and the archbishops and Bishops were desired to require each minister to intimate it from his pulpit."
- ❖ 1695. "Four hundred merks were this year granted by the Convention to be laid out in repairing the West Head, and the town of Inverkeithing was appointed to superintend the work.[15] "

On occasions, the Town Council had to press local folk into service to work on the harbour. This happened in 1630; and again in 1654 when "the strong men and women were called out to labour at these works by turns."

The Town Council also had responsibility for regulating the ferry trade, and there were problems with that as well. In 1601, our old friend Sir Robert Melville complained that his servants were being overcharged for their ferry journeys, and he appears to have secured preferential rates for them. In 1602, the city of Edinburgh attempted to impose a new tax of twelve pennies on each crossing of the Forth, but this was successfully opposed by Burntisland and Kinghorn.

---

[15] Speed suspected that this appointment of an external supervisor was necessary because of misappropriation of earlier grants.

Above: a very old photograph of the Shore (now Harbour Place). Edward Wilson Collection.

On the opposite page: Anna Crawford Briggs' impression of the Shore area. MacKenzie McGill Galleries.

In 1677, Burntisland and Kinghorn joined forces again, this time in an attempt to prevent Dysart and Kirkcaldy operating ferries across the Forth. This dispute was referred to the Privy Council and a compromise was reached, with Kirkcaldy being allowed to provide four ferry boats.

Foreign Trade

From the late 16th century, Burntisland's elite were the merchants and the ship owners and masters. Their interests were looked after by two powerful guilds, the Guildry and the Prime Gilt Society, and these organisations are discussed in Chapter VII. The granting of royal burgh status to the town consolidated the position of those leading members of society, and provided them with the opportunity to expand their operations. The law of the land greatly favoured them, for the royal burghs enjoyed a monopoly in foreign trade until 1672. Even after that date, it would have been some considerable time before the merchants in less privileged settlements were in a position to avail themselves of their newly acquired rights.

There was little specialisation in those days. Each merchant would buy and sell a wide variety of goods. Merchants from towns such as Dunfermline, Aberdour, Cupar, Leith and Edinburgh would also use the port of Burntisland and the ships which were based there.

The more enterprising merchants would often charter ships from Burntisland owners, and use them to make a quick killing. In an example from 1636, two merchant partners chartered the 'Andrew' of Burntisland and gave precise instructions to the skipper to sail immediately to Dunkirk in France, collect a cargo of salt, and deliver it to the Polish port of Danzig. This demonstrates a precise knowledge of market conditions in different countries on the part of the merchants, and their ability to respond at speed to the prospect of a sizeable profit.

Much of Burntisland's early trade was with the countries on the Baltic Sea and with Holland and Norway - although, as we see below from the case of John Brown, the town's ships plied as far south as Spain. In those days, of course, foreign trade included trade with England, and that was significant.

Examples of 16th century exports are hides, herring and cod; and, in the 17th century, coal, ale and table linen. Speed adds: "There was a considerable trade in the exportation of coals to Holland and Flanders. These were brought on horseback from Fordell and other collieries."

According to Speed, imports "consisted chiefly of ..... wood from Norway; flax from Flanders; wine from France; malt and grain from England". Speed also notes that "Beef, hides and grain were brought [by ship] from the north of Scotland. A great part of these things were for merchants of Dunfermline, Cupar, Dundee and other places."

Burntisland ships plying to and from Continental Europe were also used to provide passage to migrants in both directions. Danzig (or Gdansk) in Poland was a favourite with emigrant Scots - and also the recipient of some involuntary exiles, as related by John Blyth: "Among these passengers were many unwanted or weakly boys who, being burdensome at home for one reason or another, were shipped to Danzig to be out of the way. Many of these unfortunates died in misery, and the Scottish Government was ultimately shamed into passing prohibitive legislation."

The Loss of the 'Blessing'

When King James VI and I died in 1625, he was succeeded by his son, Charles I. Charles' English Coronation ceremony was held in February 1626, and there was some debate as to whether or not there should be a separate Scottish Coronation. Although born in Dunfermline, Charles was not keen to visit the land of his birth. He even suggested that he might be crowned

King of Scots in London. However, the Scottish Parliament insisted on a Coronation in Edinburgh. It took several years for matters to get to the stage where a date could be agreed. Eventually it was decided that the Scottish Coronation would be held on 18 June 1633 in the Abbey adjoining the Palace of Holyroodhouse.

The King and his vast entourage left London on the 10th of May, and arrived in Edinburgh five weeks later. The Privy Council had spent significant sums of money on upgrading the roads and bridges in advance of the journey. The noblemen with whom Charles stayed overnight during his journey had been ordered to ensure that their castles were, literally, fit for a King. And the same noblemen also had to feed and entertain him in the style to which he was accustomed. So great were the sums involved, that some of the nobles did not regain their financial equilibrium until years afterwards.

The same was true in Edinburgh, where no expenditure was spared. In return, the citizens were treated to a week of royal pageantry, with processions, royal banquets and a host of visiting foreign dignitaries; plus, of course, the Coronation itself.

The mood soon changed, however. After the Coronation, the King and the Scottish Parliament fell out on a number of issues. The main bones of contention were the Parliament's growing concern that the King was intent on imposing his will on Scotland, and a conviction that he was paying no attention whatsoever to what members of the Parliament were saying.

Leaving behind a disgruntled Parliament, the King set out on the 1st of July on a pre-arranged tour of royal palaces in Scotland - Linlithgow, Stirling, Dunfermline, and finally Falkland.

The return journey from Falkland to Edinburgh took place on the 10th of July 1633, and involved the crossing of the Forth from Burntisland to Leith. James Speed records the preparations in Burntisland for the royal visit (although he mistakenly refers to the King's journey as being from Leith to Burntisland, rather than in the opposite direction): "The Council ordered the officers to have a new suit of clothes, and wine confits and other eatabales to be provided for His majesty and his attendants; the streets to be cleared of middings and red; women and children to keep within doors from morning to night on the day of the King's arrival; two boats with sufficient crews to be got to ferry the King across; and lastly they resolved to admit the King and his attendants free men of the Burgh."

Cleaning and painting are activities still associated with royal visits, but it is interesting to note that in 1633 women and children had to be kept indoors and safely out of the way.

It has been suggested that the notable absence from the records of the tragedy which was to follow was the result of a cover-up to protect the King from embarrassment. We therefore do not know exactly what happened on that fateful day. However, Robert Brydon and Howard Murray have independently researched the events, and the following account is based on their conclusions from the little information available.

It appears that two Burntisland ships had been chartered for the King and his priceless possessions. One was to carry the King to a naval ship anchored in Burntisland roads. Brydon suggest that this was a man-o'-war, the 'Dreadnought', which had sailed from London as part of the Coronation plans. Murray thinks that it is unlikely that it was the 'Dreadnought', but that it was simply a ship "supplied by the Lord High Admiral, at least two masted and capable of carrying a large number of passengers".

The Burntisland ship carrying the King (and perhaps under the command of Captain A. Watson) left first and made its rendezvous with the larger vessel offshore, with the transfer of the King and some of his personnel being effected without any problems. The King then set sail for Leith, probably followed by the Burntisland vessel from which he had transferred.

In the meantime, the second Burntisland ship (the 'Blessing', which may have had Captain J. Orrock as master) set sail directly for Leith. No doubt heavily laden, she would have been less able to ride out the sudden squall which arose off Burntisland and which caused her to founder.

Left: Eric Bell's picture of the last moments of the 'Blessing.

Below: Lindsay Brydon captures the incredulity on the face of King Charles, as he witnesses the loss of the 'Blessing' from the safety of his man-o'-war.

On the opposite page: Lindsay Brydon's drawing of the disaster as it unfolds.

Howard Murray suggests that the two Burntisland vessels were between fifty and seventy feet in length and fifteen to twenty feet in breadth, with a carrying capacity of between 60 and 100 tons. They may have had the ability, as later boats had, of running cargo down a ramp into the hold.

Accounts of the tragedy give contradictory accounts of the number of lives lost. Murray estimated that the boat which sank was carrying some twenty to thirty people - a Burntisland crew of nine, with the remaining ten to twenty or so being servants of the King. There appear to have been only two survivors.

The bodies of two of those who perished were discovered in Burntisland harbour. One was identified as John Ferries, the King's cook, and James Speed records what happened following the discovery of his body.

James Speed:
1633. It is recorded as follows [that at a Burntisland Town Council meeting held on 3 August 1633] "The Bailies and Council considering that an John Ferries, servant to His Majesty, was found dead within this harbour and brought to land, who died in the boat betwixt this and Leith the time that the King His Majesty was upon the sea betwixt this and Leith, the tent day of July last; and there was found upon the said Jn Ferries the money and others following to wit, of dollars and other white money, forty five pund, twelve shillings; and of gold five twelve pund pieces and one single angel of gold 25 lib 8 shillings and 8 pennies .....
Item; ane ring of gold which was put in the council house.
Item; ane rapier sword with ane belt and hinger.
Item, ane coat and breeks of camblet.

89

The Bailies think meet that the sums bestowed on his burial be paid to the following persons, viz:-

To Andro Orrock for making graif, 16 shillings.

Item, to John White for ringing the bell, 16 shillings.

Item, to Janet Mair and Elspat Cousin for winding him, 13 shillings.

Item, to William Mitchell for washing his cot and breeks, 16 shillings.

Item, to James Brown, Taylour, 5 elns of linen to be his winding sheet, five pund, 8 shillings.

Item, to David Stirling for making his kist, 3 lib, 10 shillings.

Item, to the workmen for carrying him to the tollbooth and after to the kirk, 32 shillings.

Item, to Alexander Barnie for first spying him in the wold, 31 shillings."

August 13. Ane dollar taken out of Mr Ferries' purse to pay for the winding sheet of other man found with him.

Sept 17. The Lord Admiral desired the money and other effects which belonged to Mr Ferries to be given up to him.[16]

Dec 24. The affair of the late Mr Ferries, who it appears had been His Majesty's cook, after much negotiating was concluded by the Council obtaining, by what means is not known, the property found on him "to be given to the Kirk Session, deducting alway 40 libs to be given to the Lord Admiral for his gude will in the said money, and the Council think it expedient that the minister and Session build ane seat round the pulpit for sick aged men of the council and Session as cannot well hear the minister's voice".

Although John Ferries was described as the King's cook, this is slightly misleading. Given the amount of money he was carrying, and the elaborate funeral he was given, he would no doubt today be referred to as the King's head chef. He certainly held a senior position in the royal household.

A search for the wreck of the 'Blessing' and her potentially priceless cargo began in 1991. Following the withdrawal of an American exploration company in 1997, the search was taken over by Burntisland Heritage Group (which became Burntisland Heritage Trust the following year). Progress has been slow because the search is being carried out largely by volunteers, and also because of the very difficult underwater working conditions in the target area. At the time of writing, the search is continuing with the help of some innovative and experimental technologies.

There had been an earlier ferry disaster in 1589, also with significant royal connections. Jean Kennedy had been the faithful Matron of Honour of Mary, Queen of Scots, and had been with her right to the end, when it is said she tied the blindfold over Mary's eyes on the scaffold at Fotheringay Castle in 1587. Jean married a Melville, a relation of the Burntisland family, and became Lady Jean Melville. In 1589, King James VI summoned Lady Jean to Edinburgh to join the party who would welcome his Queen, Anne of Denmark, to her new home in Edinburgh.

So diligent was Lady Jane, that she paid no heed to the storm raging at the time, and took the first available ferry from Burntisland to Leith. In the storm, the ferry collided with another ship and sank. Some 40 people were drowned, mainly merchants and gentlewomen including Lady Jane. Also lost were priceless plate and hangings which were to have been used at the Queen's reception.

---

[16] According to Andrew Young, the Lord Admiral had anchored in Burntisland roads on 17 September, and demanded the return of Ferries' possessions. Negotiations between representatives of the Lord Admiral and the Town Council continued for over two months.

Pirates and Privateers

Burntisland certainly had its fair share of colourful shipowners and masters, and none more so than John Brown. He was the captain and part owner of a three masted Burntisland cargo ship which was active in international trade in the early years of the 17th century. The other part owners were Robert Brown (son of John), David Dowie (a Burntisland burgess) and Robert Duff of Queensferry; and they also served as members of the crew.

In 1621, John Brown set sail for Ireland with a cargo of salt, and then from Ireland to northern Spain laden with salmon. In Spain, Brown's ship was chartered by a local merchant to carry a mixed cargo of walnuts, chestnuts and iron to Cadiz on the southern coast of the country. The crew of nine were joined by three young Spaniards, who were to take over responsibility for the cargo on arrival at Cadiz.

The Browns, Dowie and Duff hatched a plot to steal the cargo. Three days into the voyage they murdered the three Spaniards, and flung their bodies into the sea. They then set a course for Holland, where they sold the nuts. They took the iron home to Burntisland and sold it there. Off they sailed again, this time on legitimate business.

It took the authorities three years to catch up with them. The ringleaders, John and Robert Brown, David Dowie and Robert Duff, were tried at Edinburgh on charges of 'murder under trust, masterful theft, robbery with violence, and piracy'. They were found guilty, and no mercy was shown. They were taken to the Market Cross

The severed heads of John and Robert Brown provide a gruesome warning to the seamen of Burntisland of the penalty for piracy and mass murder.
Pen and ink drawing by Ian McLeod.

in Edinburgh, hanged and beheaded. The heads of John Brown and Robert Brown were taken to Burntisland, and impaled on iron poles at the Green Island for all to see. The heads of Dowie and Duff were displayed at Leith.

In times of war, the government would add to the country's naval power by employing privateers. A privateer was a privately owned vessel which was authorised to seize and plunder the enemy's ships; the term was also used for the captain of such a ship. The government would issue a licence to the captain of a vessel, and in due course would take a proportion (typically ten per cent) of the spoils after a successful raid.

Several Burntisland skippers enthusiastically embraced these opportunities to pursue what was in effect legalised piracy, and gained fearsome reputations as a result of their successes.

John Blyth unearthed some fine examples of privateering by Burntisland ships during the Second Dutch War of 1665-67. Among the Burntislanders who received licences were Captain John Wemyss of the 'Wemyss Frigate' and Captain Orrock of the 'Bonaventure'. Burntisland was the main base for privateers on the Forth in this period.

Foremost among the Burntisland privateers was Captain William Ged of the 'Goodfortune'. During the two years of the war, he was credited with capturing the 'Prophet Daniel'; the 'Saint Anna' (carrying tobacco and wine); the 'Hope' (with a cargo of wine); and two further unnamed merchant vessels, one of which carried dried fish.

The Dutch were incensed by Ged's success in relieving them of their merchant ships. They were unable to stop him during the war, but when it had ended they found an opportunity to capture and jail him and his crew. Ged's wife secured their release by appealing to King Charles II to intervene.

VII   Guilds, Crafts, Markets and Fairs

In the 16th and 17th centuries, the leading citizens of Burntisland were the burgesses, and indeed this was the case up to the Burgh Reform Act of 1833.

If you were a burgess, you were technically a full member of the municipal corporation of the Royal Burgh of Burntisland. What this meant was that you were entitled to participate in the government of the burgh, as we saw in Chapter III - perhaps even seek election to the Town Council if you felt you could cope with the responsibility and if you satisfied the additional criteria. You were also entitled to certain trading and other privileges.

In exchange you had to undertake to serve the monarch and the burgh, and you had to have the resources to pay your taxes. You had to be of good character. Occasionally you would be asked to take your turn at watching and warding - standing guard on top of the town walls, to keep an eye open for undesirables who might be trying to gain entry.

Once you were a burgess, other doors opened. In addition to being eligible to join the Town Council, you could also join the town's guilds and craft associations. These were off limits - certainly in the later years - if you were not a burgess.

James Speed:
Burgesses were originally all of one rank; but about the beginning the seventeenth century the members of each particular occupation began to associate for the purpose of preventing unfreemen from working within the Burgh, and for preventing strangers from bringing in commodities for sale. The members of each craft contributed to a common fund called a box or mortification for bearing the expense of prosecuting such intruders before the Magistrates. These Associations obtained the sanction of the council on condition that each craft would undertake to support its own poor.

The guilds and associations represented specific trading and manufacturing interests in the town, and most evolved during the 17th century. Some were incorporated - that is, they were granted their own charter (known as a Seal of Cause) by the town council. This transformed a guild or association into a legal entity in its own right, giving it more clout and widening its scope to act on behalf of its members. (All these organisations, incorporated or not, are often collectively referred to as guilds, although in Scotland the correct term for an incorporated craft association is a trade incorporation.)

James Speed:
The Guildry was the principal incorporation. It began ..... with a society of traders in materials for men and women's clothes, or what was called "merchant goods". These traders claimed an exclusive right to "pack and peel" within [the] Burgh, a right which was not allowed them at that time. At intervals they renewed this claim but unsuccessfully till 1710, when they were fully incorporated with the exclusive right of trading.

Burntisland reflected the position throughout Scotland, in that the merchants and shipowners formed the most influential group. They were represented by their guild, the Guildry. Like other Fife coastal towns, Burntisland also had a Prime Gilt Society, which represented the shipmasters (captains, skippers) and seamen, and which was a force to be reckoned with. Some shipowners captained their own ships, and belonged to both the Guildry and the Prime Gilt Society. It was also common for a ship to have several part owners, all of whom would normally be eligible for membership of both organisations.

Below them in the social pecking order were the craft associations, which had to struggle to make their voices heard. As in other towns, they had to overcome the strong prejudice of the merchants against those who worked with their hands. These craft organisations are often referred to as the forerunners of trade unions, and they were to quite a large extent - but they represented the masters too, and so were also concerned with issues which were important to the bosses.

Although the Town Council seems to have been fairly sympathetic to the special pleading of the various guilds from the early 17th century onwards, the craftsmen became increasingly disillusioned at their relative lack of influence compared to the merchants and ship owners and masters.

James Speed:
..... [The] craftsmen ..... desired to be allowed to compel all workmen within the Burgh to contribute to their funds or to cease from working. The Council refused to grant this. In 1681 the Bakers and Wrights petitioned the Privy Council to compel the Town Council to grant the privileges referred to, as they called them, and to allow them to elect deacons with a right to a place in the Council. The prayer of this petition being refused, all the crafts, namely, the Masons, Wrights, Tailors, Websters, Baxters, Showemakers and Fleshers, petitioned the Court of Session to the same effect. This Court found that the Council was not obliged to grant them charters, but ordained that a visitor should be appointed by each trade to prosecute unfree or unqualified workmen before the Burgh Court, and to exact six pennies from "extraneous" workmen for every pound they earned. In 1683 the seven trades were regularly incorporated, voluntarily, I presume, by the Town Council, with the usual exclusive privileges and officers; but their deacons had not a place in the Council in right of their offices. It was agreed that in future the Council should consist of fourteen ordinary Burgesses, and one of each of the seven trades but all elected by the Council. The craftsmen were thus constituted a distinct order in the Burgh. They were proud of their "order", and stood as firmly by it as any Peer did by his, looking on all unfree men as quite an inferior class.

However, the question of the composition of the Town Council continued to cause controversy and in 1732 it was referred to arbitration. As we saw in Chapter III, it was decided that the council should continue to have 21 members - 14 (including all the magistrates) from the Guildry, and one from each of the seven incorporated trades. The trades had always coveted one of the Magistrate's offices, but this elusive prize seemed as distant as ever.

Burntisland is very privileged in this day and age to have tangible reminders of the days of the guilds. In the Parish Church are the original seats which were occupied by the guild members, and these can still be identified. Even more remarkable are the surviving painted panels representing the various guilds.

James Speed:
The Galleries [of the Parish Church] were erected in the year 1613. The greater part of these belongs to the Prime [Gilt] Society. The Guildry, Hammermen, Tailors, Bakers, Maltsmen, and Schoolmaster, have the rest. On the front of the Galleries the insignia of these trades were

painted. On the sides of the pillars opposite were texts of scripture intended to apply to the occupations of the several trades. On the other side of the pillars were inscribed the ten commandments and Lord's Prayer, with other portions of Scripture, and the apostles' Creed. Quaint representations of men with sextants and antique ships on the front of the Sailor's loft, were objects of curiosity. The Merchants had their inexplicable figure 4.

Speed goes on to lament the fact that the panels in the church were painted over in 1822. This obliteration was part of a cheap renovation of the church following a fire in the north gallery, and was carried out at a time when funds were low. We are indeed fortunate that, during a subsequent renovation in 1907, the possibility of restoring the panels was examined. Restoration was declared to be feasible, and it fell to Andrew Young, the local artist, photographer and historian, to take the work forward. Leading citizens sponsored the restoration of individual panels, and Young worked on this task, as and when time permitted, up to his death in 1925.

Young had always been puzzled about the fate of the weavers' panel, which had been referred to by Mary Somerville in her autobiographical writings. Many years later, in 1973, it was discovered in a house in Kirkcaldy, along with one of the Prime Gilt Society panels. They had been removed for safe keeping during the 1822 renovations. Both were restored and returned to the church.

The panels are a fascinating reminder of times long gone, when society was organised along quite different lines. In addition, those which carry illustrations provide unique examples of 17th century art - not fine art perhaps, but competently executed and truly representative of the period. Some of the panels, with brief descriptions, are illustrated on pages 96 and 97.

As we have seen, the guilds existed to protect and promote the interests of their members. Their activities included lobbying for higher prices; monitoring the quality of goods produced; trying to prevent outsiders and non-members from selling goods within the town; taking offenders to court; and supporting members and their dependents who had fallen on hard times. Their revenues came from subscriptions; fines on their members; renting out their spare seats in the church; and renting mortcloths (expensive cloaks, often of trimmed velvet, for covering the coffin of a person who had died, prior to burial).

Each guild elected a head (called the deacon) and a treasurer (called the boxmaster). The boxmaster looked after the guild's box, which was usually kept in his house. As there were no banks, the box was where the guild's money and important documents were held. It was usually a stout wooden trunk, with two or three locks. The multiple locks were a safeguard against fraud. There were several keyholders and no individual could gain access to the contents by himself.

The photographs on the following two pages show some of the painted guild panels in Burntisland Parish Church. Most if not all of them are 17th century.

Left hand page: (from left to right) a late 17th century vessel, possibly a Government despatch ship; a favourite 17th century motto; one from the late 17th century; a sailor fathoming a rope; a shipmaster with astrolabe and cross-staff. Ian Archibald.

Right hand page: (top left) a 17th century merchant brig; (top right) one of the Guildry (merchants') panels; (middle left) a shipmaster measuring the altitude of the sun; (middle right) depiction of a sea battle; (bottom left) a master mariner with astrolabe and cross-staff; (bottom right) a brig of the mid 17th century. Gavin Anderson.

Left: the joint insignia of the smiths, wrights and masons. Andrew Young.

Right: the Weavers' Box. Andrew Young.

There follows a brief description of each of Burntisland's guilds. They all had their own seats in the Parish Church, except the Wrights (who shared with the Hammermen) and the Hirers.

Guildry   This was the most important of Burntisland's guilds, and represented the merchants, shopkeepers, shipowners and shipmasters. There was a degree of overlap with the Prime Gilt Society, which represented seamen of all classes. The Guildry could trace its origins back to at least 1606, and was probably in existence well before that. In 1611 it had only ten members, but expanded considerably in later years. It was incorporated in 1710. It invested its funds in local property purchases and in loans to the Town Council. It was wound up in 1860, probably as a result of its waning influence following the passage of the Burgh Reform Act of 1833.

Prime Gilt Society   Described as powerful and wealthy, but secretive, it latterly represented shipowners, shipmasters, sailors and ships' carpenters. Its name derived from "prymgilt", the term for a sum of money paid to the master and crew of a ship for the loading and care of a cargo - a sum which came to include a percentage levied for insurance against ill health and unemployment The Society was probably formed in the 16th century. It was active in the Burntisland property market, buying and selling; and it provided loans on the security of property. Unfortunately, many of the Society's records were destroyed in a fire at the home of the then boxmaster, James Morrison, in 1845. The Society was never incorporated.

Hammermen   This guild took under its wing, not just the smiths and other metal workers, but also the masons, slaters and coopers. It had a very close relationship with the Wrights, with whom it effectively amalgamated. The Hammermen and the Wrights were individually incorporated in 1683, and they elected separate deacons - but they shared the same box and held joint meetings.

Wrights   Carpenters and other wood workers. See Hammermen.

Tailors   Incorporated in 1683, it became the most infamous of the guilds. On Michaelmas (29 September) every year, the tailors rented out their seats in the Parish Church, and used the proceeds to have what Andrew Young described as "a great spree", from which it would have taken them days to recover. The result was that there was no money to maintain the seats, which fell into a serious state of disrepair. The Kirk Session lent them money for the repairs, but they were unable to pay the interest and had to surrender their seats.

Weavers   As described above, their panel was rescued from a house in Kirkcaldy in 1973. It is the only guild of whose box we have a photograph. The guild was incorporated in 1683.

Cordiners   The cordiners or shoemakers were also incorporated in 1683, and we have a list of their names at that time - Michael Setoun, Alexander Orrock, Walter Adams, William Moyes, James Gardiner, William Mitchelson, John Crawford, Andrew Robinson, John Orrock, William Blankiter, James Anderson, John Young, and George Walkethusent.

Fleshers   The fleshers or butchers were another of the seven crafts incorporated in 1683.

Baxters   The baxters or bakers were also incorporated in 1683.

Maltmen   They were never incorporated, but they could trace their origins back to at least 1608 and had their own seats in the church. Their malt kilns were in the area between the north side of the High Street and the East Broomhill.

Hirers   Numerous at one time, they were frequently in trouble for hiring out their post-horses to excursionists on Sundays. They were never incorporated.

Although they are from a later date (1835), the following membership figures give an indication of the relative strengths of the seven trade incorporations - Hammermen and Wrights (combined) - 12; Tailors - 5; Weavers - 2; Fleshers - 1; Shoemakers - 12; Bakers - 4.[17]

Market and Fair Days

As mentioned in Chapter III, Burntisland's market cross was situated in the centre of the High Street, west of the present library, and its position is now indicated by a cobbled marker. A town's 'market cross' was not necessarily in the shape of a cross, and the only clue we have about Burntisland's is Speed's comment: "The cross was about the middle of the High Street, at which there was some kind of wooden fabric and the pillar at which offenders were exposed." There was certainly some structure in the middle of the High Street, because 'Cross' is marked on the map of 1746 on page 32. The cross was often where sinners were ordered to display penitence, as shown in the illustration on page 39.

Although the High Street still follows the same line today, the features in the market cross area would have been quite different in the 17th century. Beside the actual 'cross' there would have been a small building called the tron house or cross house (referred to in the records, and probably the "wooden fabric" to which Speed refers). Inside the tron house would be the public weighing machine. Where the Burgh Chambers now stand, at the corner of the High Street and Kirkgate, were the shambles (abattoir) and an area for the traders from out of town to display their produce.

The local traders would display and sell their wares at their booths in the High Street, and also at the market cross on the appointed market days. In the early 17th century, the sale of cakes, oatmeal, butter, eggs, cheese, meat, fish, candles and beer was strictly regulated, and the prices were fixed by the Town Council. The Council had gone to a great deal of trouble to create an elaborate web of rules and regulations relating to trade within the town, and did its best to ensure that these were followed to the letter.

---

[17] Source: Report of the Royal Commission on Municipal Corporations in Scotland (1835).

A Scottish Fair by Andrew Young (1910). The painting is based on the annual summer fairground on Burntisland Links. Young is reputed to have created it as a wedding present for the couple who are pictured centre stage. Kirkcaldy Museum & Art Gallery.

Ian McLeod's watercolour depicting the first horse race from Burntisland to Pettycur in 1652. Burntisland Heritage Trust Collection.

For example, the market days for perishables such as bread were Mondays, Tuesdays, Wednesdays and Saturdays. On these days, traders from outside the town were also allowed in to sell at the fixed prices, but under no circumstances were they allowed to stray far from the market cross.

The brewers were a group who were often falling foul of the law, usually for selling over-priced ale. On one occasion, 61 of them were fined for this transgression.

James Speed - a local merchant himself, although at a much later date - was not very complimentary about the quality of goods supplied by local craftsmen.

James Speed:
The craftsmen were employed in making commodities for the use of the inhabitants of the town and neighbourhood. They seem, however, to have had little skill in their trades, for it required all their vigilance to prevent the workmen of the neighbouring towns from intruding on them. The Weavers, Tailors and Butchers of Aberdour were a sore cause of annoyance. When any important piece of work was to be done, workmen were brought from Dundee, Dunfermline, and other places to execute it.

It seemed at times as if the local craftsmen were spending most of their time looking out for competing intruders, rather than turning out good qualityarticles of their own.

As late as 1835, some of the local craftsmen in the town were still attempting to justify the anti-competition rules and regulations, but the Burgh Trading Act of 1846 abolished these for ever.

James Speed:
Fairs and Markets. The feasts of St Peter and St John were appointed fair days. The first is still held on the 29 June old style (10 July). The other had been long discontinued. Besides the trade prosecuted on these occasions horse and foot races and other amusements were instituted.
..... 1654. Race. During the gloomy time of national and local oppression[17], the Council instituted a horse race to be run from the East Port to Pettycur on the 29 June (10 July) being St Peter's fair, for a silver cup of 10 ounces weight. No horse was allowed to run above the value of 300 merks. At the same time it was attempted to establish a market for the sale of cattle, but it did not succeed. The race was kept up till about the year 1812.

Subsequent writers have dated the first horse race as taking place in 1652. And Andrew Young, writing in 1924, reported that the silver cup which Speed mentions was at that time in the possession of a Burntisland family who had emigrated to Australia.

However, these two snippets from James Speed's notes do give us the origins of what we now call Market Day or Games Day. St Peter's Day is still the 29th of June, but the Burntisland fair has migrated to the third Monday in July.

A large number of market traders continue to descend on the town on that day, keeping the tradition alive. And the horse race of 1652 has evolved into the other major event held on the third Monday of July, namely Burntisland Highland Games. There may no longer be a horse race, but the current full programme of events always attracts a bumper crowd.

---

[18] The time of Cromwell's occupation.

Depending on the weather, between 30,000 and 50,000 folk visit the town on Market Day, to enjoy the market and the games - and also the summer fairground, which is resident on the Links from late May to late August every year.

VIII   Sins and Sinners

From the 16th century on, the Magistrates of the Town Council of Burntisland were responsible for law and order. They tried and punished offenders, sometimes with the assistance of a jury. The magistrates were appointed by the Town Council from among their own ranks, and in particular the merchants, shipowners and shipmasters. The office of magistrate was one which the craftsmen aspired to, but which they were never permitted to hold.

James Speed tells us that "At Burntisland the public peace was maintained by the ordinary constables. These were composed of Burgess households and young men of respectable station. They exercised a moral authority in the discharge of their duty which we shall look for in vain in a paid police force."

On the whole, Burntisland appears to have been a relatively law-abiding place in the 17th century. The cells in the tolbooth are described as being under-used, certainly as far as the housing of local criminals was concerned. Probably that was one of the advantages of the fact that Burntisland was a walled town. Known wrongdoers could be kept out. In 1669, "owing to the increase of the number of beggars and robbers, watching and warding were strictly enforced on the inhabitants."

The magistrates also had the power to expel any residents who committed serious crimes - no doubt to the detriment of Aberdour and other neighbouring settlements.

Around 1598, according to Speed, the council ordered the town to be "purged of slanderous, suspicious and unprofitable members, which was done". In 1633, "Thomas Phin was banished for ever for being a drunken beast, and for so misbehaving himself that the lieges cannot live in peace for him."

In later years, lest anyone try to protect undesirables, "those harbouring vagabonds, thieves, strangers or those suspected of scandal, were ordered to pay a fine of forty shillings".

Robert Livingstone quotes another case of banishment, this time from 1740. The magistrates, William Greig, John Ritchie junior and Patrick Angus, summoned "Marion Brown spouse to Charles Orrock Land Labourer in Burntisland who voluntarily enacted bound and obliged herself forthwith to remove furth of this burgh and never return hereto or the territories thereof under the pain of a month's imprisonment and feeding on bread and water and standing in the Juggs and being whyped thro the town each week and again banished and undergo the like punishment so oft as she returns." We are not told what Marion's crime was, but it seems unlikely that she would have returned to Burntisland, given the further punishments which awaited her.

For some reason, the period around 1620 was an unusually troubled one. James Speed commented: "Crimes and offences greatly prevailed in the town about this time. They are described as bloodwits, turbulances, profane swearing, opposing the Magistrates, abusing the minister, and also some unnamable crimes. It seemed as if society had fallen into barbarism."

Clearly the burden of feeding the prisoners in this period was becoming too much for the town, for the Magistrates decreed that the expense of supporting prisoners should be borne "by the parties at whose instance they were incarcerated. Thirteen pennies daily was the prescribed allowance (1½d sterling)."

There were, of course, a number of serious crimes committed by local folk. John Brown, Robert Brown and David Dowie, who engaged in mass murder and piracy and who are discussed in Chapter VI, at least had the decency to commit their sins well away from Burntisland.

Within the town itself, there was a small number of recorded murders in the 17th century.

Around 1608, an English ship's captain by the name of Wilson was murdered in the town. Wilson's brother then swore a revenge killing of the first Scotsman he met on his travels. We do not know the outcome of the threat, although one man reported a narrow escape when he met the brother on the Isle of Crete.

Another 17th century case was that of Alexander Johnstone of Newbigging who committed the "cruel murder" of his neighbour, James Johnstone.

In 1660, in the last days of the English occupation, Alexander Boswell, a Kirkcaldy skipper, was killed in Burntisland by Peter Bettwood, a trooper of Captain Fermer's company. After examining witnesses, the Bailies surrendered the accused to the army, although his fate is not recorded.

James Speed:

1666. Murder. A murder was committed by William Moncrieff, Tailor, on William Brown of Dunbar, by stabbing him with a whanger. The Bailies found that they had not authority to try the accused, and therefore applied to his Grace the Commissioner, and the Lord Justice General for advice. The Council desired that if the said William be convicted, he should suffer here. By a Privy Council warrant he was taken to Edinburgh, and there is nothing further recorded regarding him.

Raised tempers in the Town Council chamber could lead to serious problems. In the following example, it was fortunate that no more than words were exchanged.

James Speed:

1598. A Riotous Councillor. There were many disorders committed in the town at this time, for instance, a Town Councillor abused the Bailies in the Council house, and on being ordered to go to ward, refused to surrender, drew his whanger, threw down his glove, and challenged them to single combat, and then betook himself to his own house from the "windock" of which he continued the wordy warfare. For all which offences he was brought before a Head court, fined in ten merks, ordained to behave well in future, and to ask pardon of the Council on his knees in the church, after the Wednesday preaching.

As this shows, it was not just the working classes who misbehaved. On another occasion, a group of belligerent burgesses, led by James Young, a tailor, assaulted Town Clerk Andrew Wilson with "fauldit neives and feit and great stanes". They then turned on Wilson's companion, Bailie Ged, and "upbraided and assaulted him, took him by the gorgit and baird and ruggit a grite part of the hair out of his baird, rave his overla fra his craig" and struck him. The burgesses were arrested. Young was ordered to be detained in Edinburgh Tolbooth, at his own expense and during the Privy Council's pleasure. The others were acquitted.

The Role of the Church

The church had its own code of conduct, and members were expected to live their lives according to that code. Transgressors were summoned to appear before the Kirk Session, which was in effect a minor court in its own right. The sin of fornication received much attention, and old Kirk Session minute books are crammed with references to hearings involving the guilty parties, both male and female.

The riotous councillor of 1598.
Drawings by Douglas Gray.

James Speed:
During the whole of the seventeenth century whether prelacy or presbyterianism was in the ascendant, strict discipline was exercised by the Session over the inhabitants of the parish. Those convicted of scolding, flyting, profane swearing and minor offences against good morals were called before the Session and rebuked there or before the congregation. In aggravated cases they were required to ask pardon of those they had offended or injured, sometimes on their knees in presence of the congregation. Those convicted of having illegitimate children or of other grave offences were ordained to sit a certain number of Sabbaths on an elevated seat at the south east pillar of the church, in some cases in a white sheet. The number of Sabbaths during which the penitents appeared in this dress were more or less, according to the degree of the offence, but sometimes extended to twenty six. The Romish confessional could show nothing more disgusting, as I imagine, than the examination of the accused persons on such occasions, as detailed in the Kirk Session records.

So keen were the Kirk Session to find wrongdoers and punish them, that they appointed searchers, a rather sinister form of snooper, to identify culprits and inform on them.

James Speed:

Searchers. There was a certain number of persons who had a seat appropriated to them in the church, called "searchers". These informed against persons suspected of improper conduct, especially those guilty of profane swearing, drinking to excess, promiscuous dancing, but more particularly Sabbath breaking. Now, one is accused of "vaging" in the fields, at the shore or at the Castle Bank on Sabbath; another is found toasting bread at the fire, or bringing in water on that day; and again one is accused of absenting himself from public worship. For these and similar offences the perpetrators were ordered to appear before the Session to repent and be rebuked. Those who failed to obey were held to be contumacious, and were turned over to the civil power to be imprisoned or banished. The letting of horses or freighting of ferry-boats on Sabbath without leave from the magistrates was forbidden on pain of forfeiting the hire or freight, which was given to the poor. Occasionally a fine was exacted, by way of indulgence I presume, for leave to commit the offence of hiring horses or freighting boats on Sunday. Persons coming to reside in the town were required to bring certificates of character from the minister of the place they had left. Uncertificated persons were refused liberty to reside in the town. About the year 1670 on its being found that the Magistrates were not sufficiently compliant in such cases, and that their authority extended only to banishment from the town, application was made to the Sheriff for the appointment of a Bailie Depute or Kirk Bailie, as he was called, to have power to banish contumacious offenders from the whole parish. The application was granted, but I have seen no notice of its having been renewed.

The Kirk Session did not limit their enquiries to open offenders, but instructed investigations into the private affairs of all persons whom they suspected of doing what they considered wrong.

As Speed indicated in the above extract, the Kirk Session and the town magistrates worked closely together. If the Kirk Session believed that a case was too serious for it to deal with, it would refer it to the magistrates. Examples of really serious cases were those involving bestiality, sodomy and incest. Uncommunicative fornicators were also referred to the magistrates, as in a 1665 case mentioned by Speed: "Three women were imprisoned till they told who were the fathers of their illegitimate children."

Slanderers could also be referred to the magistrates. In 1602, Gill Watson "was convicted by the Council of calling the pastor a Devil, and ordained to stand at the cross with a paper on her head with an inscription in large letters setting forth her

The three single mothers about to be jailed in the tolbooth. Each wears a large placard with the word 'FORNICATOR'. Pen and ink drawing by Keli Clark.

offence; and to stand with the same ornament at the north east pillar of the Kirk during the forenoon preaching." In 1656, Janet Haldane "was ordained to stand at the cross with 'a vile slanderer' inscribed on a paper on her head, for slandering Isobel Burnet." Janet is featured in the illustration on page 39.

The Town Council would frequently give legislative backing to the church, by passing laws prohibiting moral transgressions. Speed gives the following examples.

James Speed:

1608. Religious Observance. Immediately after the town was considered free from the plague, the Council set about enforcing attendance on religious ordinances, apparently as an expression of their gratitude to God for the deliverance. All persons were enjoined to attend the service of the church on Sundays and other days, especially they required that the Tuesday's preaching be better attended, and the Sabbath better kept. They therefore ordained that all persons absent from the church on Sabbath shall be warded in the Tron House for twelve hours, "without meat or drink but bread and water", or pay a fine of twenty shillings for the first offence, thirty for the second, forty for the third, all without prejudice to the censure of the Kirk Session.

..... c1655. Profanity. The laws against "profane swearing, cursing, scolding, mocking of piety, filthy speaking, drinking to excess and compelling others to drink", were ordered by the Magistrates to be put in execution, "and that without prejudice to the censures of the Kirk".

..... c1667. Sabbath. At this time repeated orders were issued by the Council for enforcing the strict observance of the Sabbath. No boats were allowed to cross the ferry, nor any horses to be hired for inland journeys without leave from the Bailies. These regulations continued in force till towards the end of last century[18].

..... 1689. Act against Profanity. The council enacted as follows:- "Albeit that by several Acts of Parliament, cursing, swearing, excessive drinking, profaning the Sabbath, mocking the worship of God and the free exercise thereof, are prohibited, yet these sins abound in this town, therefore it is ordained that those guilty thereof shall pay for swearing, drinking and Sabbath breaking twelve shillings; for mocking the worship of God, forty shillings."

..... 1695. Profanity etc. The Council issued an order to the following effect: "considering that the profanation of the Lords-day, profane swearing, absence from public worship and other immoralities are prohibited by several Acts of Parliament, ... which Acts also forbid the keeping of markets or prosecuting any kind of trade on that day, under the penalty of ten pounds Scots, ... ordains that persons frequenting ale houses on Sabbath, except for travel or refreshment, shall pay for the first fault three pounds or be put six hours in the gongs, increasing the penalty for repeated faults till they are to be put in jail, there to remain till they find security for their better behaviour." ..... [In addition, the Council] "prohibit all persons within this Burgh to labour on the Lord's day, or to be found in the streets or to go in companies or 'vage' to the shore or Castle Brae, West Shore or fields on that day or any time therof, or to go to ale houses or taverns". They further ordained that no person should bring more than a pint of water from the wells on Sabbath. Parents and masters were to be held answerable for their children and servants; and those who were unable to pay the fines were to be punished in their bodies according to the "merit of the fault".

In Scotland, up until as recently as 1962, you could buy a drink on a Sunday only if you were a 'bona fide traveller'. This was an enduring legacy from earlier days, and was rigorously

---

[19] The 18th century.

enforced in 17th century Burntisland, when the Kirk Session went to great lengths to keep non-travellers out of the alehouses. The Session were greatly distressed when they learned that there was "ane great abuse in this toune by some who makes it thair ordinarie practice and custome after Sermones to conveen at the shoar and then to go to taverns and thair tipple", and the kirk elders were instructed to seek out the sinners and report them to the authorities.

Witchcraft

In the 17th century, the persecution of witches was common throughout Europe. This persecution was not confined to Protestant countries, but it was the churches in those countries which displayed the worst excesses. And Calvinist Scotland was at the forefront in seeking out those described as the 'malevolent and potent agents of the devil'.

The Scottish Parliament set the scene in 1563, by decreeing that the practice of witchcraft would be punishable by execution. For the following 100 years the Church of Scotland, in association with the civil authorities, implemented the law - sometimes enthusiastically and sometimes grudgingly. Estimates of the number of people, mainly women, who were executed for witchcraft in Scotland vary considerably, from 1,300 to 4,500.

Most of the guilty women were in fact entirely innocent of any wrongdoing. They might be elderly and a little wandered, or perhaps eccentric in some way. They were often what we now call bad neighbours, and prone to cursing and swearing. But they could be accused of witchcraft on the basis of a single complaint to the Church by a local person with a grudge against them.

The zealousness of the persecution was determined by both the prevailing national climate and local factors. In Fife, the witch hunts were concentrated in the southern parishes, in particular Culross, Inverkeithing, Burntisland, Kinghorn, Kirkcaldy and Dysart. Many local landowners like Sir Robert Melville of Rossend Castle were keen to see local witches being tracked down and dealt with.

Some ministers gained a fearsome reputation for encouraging their flocks to seek out and report anyone who might be a witch. One such was the notorious Rev John Smith, Minister of Burntisland from 1643 to 1649. John Blyth speculated on his influence: "This man, with his sinister reputation, must almost certainly have been a grim figure as he passed through the streets of our town. One can imagine the children shrinking from his presence, and terrified old women hastening whenever possible from his sight." Such was the power exercised by fanatical ministers three to four hundred years ago, and the climate of fear which was created.

The more eccentric women of Burntisland would have breathed a sigh of relief when Cromwell captured the town in 1651 - simply because he imposed a near prohibition of witchcraft trials during the period of occupation.

John Blyth did some research on witchcraft in Burntisland, but was hampered by the absence of records from so long ago. However, his limited information does give us a flavour of what happened here during those turbulent times.

In 1648, the unfortunate Janet Brown of Burntisland was put on trial by the Commissioners - a panel of men drawn from the local establishment for the express purpose of conducting witchcraft trials. It was normal practice for a suspect to be interrogated prior to the actual trial. This typically involved forms of torture, perhaps the use of thumbscrews or sleep deprivation. Another grotesque practice was witch-pricking, the insertion of a long pin of wire into the body to test for pain sensitivity and the presence of blood. So common was this operation that a new profession - witch-prickers - came into being, comprising men skilled in the operation and interpretation.

Burntisland's Janet Brown was subjected to witch-pricking. Her alleged crime? - the rather unlikely one of having a meeting with the Devil who appeared as a man at the back of the Broomhlls, who was "at wanton play" with two other women, and who "vanished away like a whirlwind". But before he left, the Devil had made a mark on Janet's right arm. This mark - probably in fact a mole or birthmark - was the target for the witch-pricking, and the men who carried it out were the Ministers of Dysart and Auchterderran. They must have been satisfied with their findings, for Janet was found guilty and executed.

Those convicted of witchcraft were typically ordered to be taken out, bound to a stake or chained to a rock, strangled until dead, and then burnt in pitch until they were ashes. This is probably how Janet Brown met her end. We cannot be sure where these atrocities were carried out, although it is likely to have been in the Lammerlaws area. No doubt Janet's burning would have presented a fine public spectacle.

To make matters even worse for the families of those found guilty, they were held liable for the expenses incurred by the authorities in processing the witchcraft cases.

Janet Allan meets her end at the Lammerlaws.
Pen and ink drawing by Ian McLeod.

Another Burntisland witch, Janet Allan, had met an even grimmer end in 1598. It is likely that she was one of the minority who were burned alive. This punishment was reserved for the more troublesome cases.

James Speed:
Robert Brown accused Janet Allan of having caused the death of his son by witchcraft. The Magistrates refused to interfere unless security were given that they would be relieved of the expense of trying and of executing her, if found guilty. The required security being given, Janet was tried by a jury of fifteen persons, found guilty, and sentenced to be "burnt quick". The sentence, however, was not executed, for what cause is not recorded, for soon after she was again accused of a similar crime, and again sentenced to be burnt.

John Blyth reckoned that the last witchcraft trial in Burntisland took place in 1672. It is also the best documented case, and illustrates the ridiculous lengths that the authorities would go to, to try to secure a conviction.

The woman on trial was Elspeth Finlay, who appears to have been a domestic servant to one William Anderson. Mr Anderson sent Elspeth to the local ale merchant to get him a pint of ale. On the way, Elspeth came across Margaret Cowper, who encouraged her to steal a baby's hair ribbon - which she did. On another occasion, Margaret Cowper poured some water on one of Elspeth's fingers, and a tall stranger wearing black clothes and a blue bonnet then put his cold hand on Elspeth's hand. The third piece of evidence was that Elspeth had stolen a drinking vessel from Alexander Ged. At her interrogation, Elspeth admitted that she did not pray to God; and her mother confirmed that her behaviour had always been something of a problem.

That was more or less the substance of the accusations. The accounts of the later stages of this case have been lost. However, we do know that one of the members of the commission which investigated Elspeth's case was the Kinghorn Cyclops. He was minister of that parish and another notorious witch hunter, and he had only one eye. To conceal his disfigurement, he wore a black mask which emphasised the penetrating stare emanating from his solitary good eye.

The case apparently dragged on for many months, with the commissioners unable to reach agreement. But we do know that in the end Elspeth was acquitted, because she is recorded as successfully applying to the church for a reference in 1674.

The trial of the North Berwick witches in 1595 is one of Scotland's best known cases. The principal accusation was that the witches had created a great storm, with the aim of sinking the ship bringing King James VI and his new bride home from Denmark in 1590. The king actively involved himself in the trial, and wrote a book on the evils of witchcraft.

James' son, King Charles I, apparently inherited his father's belief in witchcraft, and applied it to his own misfortune - the sinking of his chartered ferry off Burntisland in 1633, which is described in Chapter VI. According to the Privy Council records for 1634, a group of Lancashire witches were accused of, among other things, causing the shipwreck. Several of them were taken to London for investigation.

The statutes against witchcraft were finally repealed in 1736.

We will never know how many innocent citizens of Burntisland were the victims of judicial murder by the church and civil authorities in God's name. Here are the names of nine of them, including those already mentioned.

- ❖ 1597 - Janet Smith (strangled and burned)
- ❖ 1598 - Janet Allan (burned alive)
- ❖ 1648 - Janet Brown, and probably Isobel Gardner and Janet Thomson (strangled and burned)
- ❖ 1649 - Janet Murray, Elspeth Ronaldson and Agnes Waterson (strangled and burned)
- ❖ 1650 - Elspeth Austin (strangled and burned)

Postscript

by Fraser Gold and Iain Sommerville

This book was conceived with the primary aim of bringing James Speed's notes on the history of Burntisland to a wider audience. That developed into a more ambitious project, to produce a history of Burntisland which would cover the period to the Union of Parliaments and which would be in a form which would appeal to 21st century readers. We hope the end product achieves these aims.

As we have seen, Burntisland's history illustrates so many aspects of the wider history of Scotland. The development of towns and town organisations in the Middle Ages was most marked along the eastern seaboard or estuaries. Although these towns were very small by today's standards, they handled the most significant trade of the time, which was across the North Sea. The importance of Burntisland's role is clearly demonstrated by the fact that the town became the second port on the Forth estuary, after Leith.

As trade developed, merchant interests challenged the feudal lairds of castle and abbey everywhere, so Burntisland's difficulties with Sir Robert Melville and Dunfermline Abbey were typical. The merchant guilds then jealously tried to hold their privileged position against the craft guilds, as illustrated in Chapter VII.

The various religious changes and upheavals which were experienced in Scotland were again mirrored in the history of Burntisland, and are brought to life in the sometimes tragic and occasionally comic incidents which Speed and others have recorded. Educational provision was almost universally as haphazard as it was in Burntisland.

The early growth of the town, fuelled by North Sea trade and the ferry link to Edinburgh, brought a number of royal visitors to Burntisland over the years. The hazards of navigation on the Forth were appreciated, and harbour works were constantly receiving attention. The tragedy of the 'Blessing' must have been a stark indication that the attractive waters of the firth were not always benign.

We have of course left the reader, rather abruptly, at the beginning of the 18th century. Burntisland had by then risen from humble beginnings to become a port of national significance. It had earned its title, 'Port of Grace'.

In the 18th century, the Jacobite risings of 1715 and 1745 provided some excitement, as did the 1738 secession from the Church of Scotland. But in general Burntisland remained in the post-Union doldrums for much of the 18th century.

The 19th century, however, saw significant economic improvement based on three developments - the coming of the railway in 1847; the massive increase in coal exports; and the further development of the sea links to Granton for both passengers and freight.

Unfortunately for Burntisland, the opening of the Forth Bridge in 1890 took away much of the passenger traffic to Granton. And the development of new docks at Methil in the 1880s provided stiff competition for the Burntisland coal exporting operations.

The boom times returned in the early 20th century, with the opening of the aluminium works and the shipyard at the end of the First World War. By that time, Burntisland was also making a name for itself as a holiday destination and a venue for day trippers.

In more recent years, Burntisland, like other towns in Scotland, has had to adjust to changing industrial patterns, and to the availability of inexpensive holidays abroad. The shipyard closed in 1969, and the aluminium works in 2002. Burntisland still plays host to holidaymakers and day trippers, but not in the numbers of former years.

However, no-one can deny the town's beautiful location. Between three and four hundred dwellings will soon cover the site of the aluminium works, and the new residents will provide a welcome boost to local businesses. Large sums have been committed for improvements to the town centre. The first class sea and rail facilities offer great potential. At the time of writing, in October 2004, the prospects are good.

Above: Burntisland from the Binn. Bill Kirkhope.

Below: Burntisland from the Black Rock. Ian Archibald.

Above: the original volume, held in Fife Council Archive Centre.
On the opposite page: an extract. Helen Mabon.

Appendix A - James Speed's Notes on the History of Burntisland

James Speed's original notes are held in the Fife Council Archive Centre in Markinch. They are contained in a leather-bound foolscap volume entitled "Documents relating to the history of Burntisland, Transcribed by Alexander Foster. 1869", and described as "The property of The Magistrates & Town Council of Burntisland". It contains "Notes relating to the Royal Burgh of Burntisland chiefly compiled from the Burgh Records by James Speed" - 235 pages in Foster's fine copperplate handwriting. As Speed died in 1867, and the volume is dated 1869, it is clear that Foster decided to create a permanent record from notes left by Speed. We do not know exactly when the original notes were written.

The first section of the notes (14 pages of the original volume) is a helpful description of Scottish royal burghs, couched in general terms. The second section (60 pages) is a brief history of the Royal Burgh of Burntisland. The remainder of the volume (161 pages) comprises notes by James Speed, based on material in the Burntisland Burgh records for the period 1596 to 1708.

There is no indication why Speed stopped at 1708. It is possible that it had been his original intention to carry on to a much later date. Perhaps ill health or his premature death brought the project to an end.

James Speed's notes were transcribed by Helen Mabon, and are reproduced in their entirety in this appendix. With the exception of a few minor editing and formatting changes, they are as they appear in the manuscript volume. Where possible, apparent inconsistencies in the original text are clarified by the use of footnotes.

Broadly speaking, when a year is mentioned in a sub-heading, that year relates to all the notes until a year is once again mentioned in a sub-heading. But that is not always the case, and some care and a degree of personal interpretation are required at times. When a month and day are mentioned at the beginning of an entry, this is usually the date of the council record, rather than the date of the event described.

The more obscure words and terms are included in the glossary at Appendix B. The terms and conventions relating to currencies are described in Appendix C.

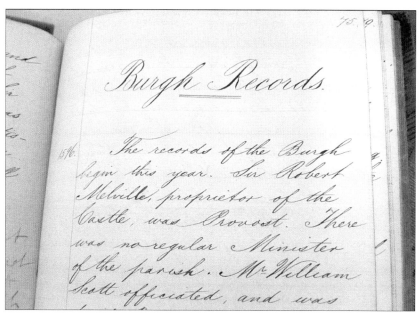

Notes Relating to the Royal Burgh of Burntisland Chiefly Compiled from the Burgh Records by James Speed

ROYAL BURGHS

During the twelfth century the inhabitants of certain towns were endowed by the Kings of Scotland with important municipal privileges, constituting these places Free Burghs Royal. The number of such towns at the end of that century was about eighteen, which number was from time to time increased by new erections, till at the period of the union of the Kingdoms they amounted to sixty six, exclusive of some that had renounced the right of sending Commissioners to Parliament.

The privileges conferred on these places were in some respects similar to those conferred on the incorporated communities of France by Louis VI, and in others to those possessed by the boroughs of England subsequent to the Norman conquest.

On the introduction of the feudal system into Scotland, each Royal Burgh came to be considered a vassal of the Crown. The community was authorised to administer justice and to manage the common property. The permanent inhabitants were all freemen. If a bondman lived a year and a day in a Royal Burgh "unchallenged", he could not be claimed by his master, but, unless he was the King's bondman, was ever afterwards free.

These Burghs were the only places in Scotland where the lower classes of the people in early times had anything approaching to civil liberty, or whose trade or the industrial arts could be prosecuted without being subject to the capricious interference and exactions of the nobility and barons. Deriving their immunities from the Sovereign, the inhabitants of the Burghs were generally disposed to protect him against the aggressions of the higher nobles.

In the year 1141, David the first, by a Charter dated from Newcastle, conferred on the Royal Burgesses of Scotland the exclusive right of trading in staple wares. These wares were chiefly cloth, wine, hides, wool and salt. These Burgesses claimed also the sole right of prosecuting foreign trade. Each Burgess paid a sum of money on his admission to the incorporation, which varied in amount according to circumstances; but he could not enjoy the corporate privileges unless he was possessed of a rood of "bigget land", or acquired it within a year of his admission. It was for some time a question whether a person on his admission as a Burgess in any one Burgh, was to be held as free of all the other Burghs of Scotland; but it was at length decided that he was free only in that in which he had been admitted.

The Burgess, according to the letter of the law, could sell his land to whom he pleased, if he had acquired it by purchase; but if he had obtained it by inheritance, he was obliged to offer it at three head counts to his nearest of kin. If the nearest of kin refused to take the land, the Burgess might dispose of it as he pleased; but if the nearest of kin took it, he was, without reference to the price paid, obliged to see that the disposer was ever afterwards provided with "meat, drink and clothes, white or grey".

Burgesses were obliged to serve the King in his wars, whether foreign or civil. In the reign of Robert the second, each Burgess was obliged to provide himself with a horse for military service, of the value of twenty shillings, equal in respect to the silver it contained to three pounds and eight shillings of our present money, but in exchangeable value to about eighteen pounds. But Burgesses were occasionally subjected to less honourable service, such as was usually exacted of bondmen. Till the end of the fifteenth century the social position of Burgesses was indeed little above that of bondmen. They, however, had the right of going armed, and of entering into holy orders – rights which bondmen did not possess, nor could acquire without the permission of their masters. In some other respects Burgesses and bondmen were reckoned of the same degree; for instance, if the tutor or guardian of a female ward though she were the daughter of one of no higher station than that of a vavasour or subvassal, allowed her to marry a Burgess or bondman, he was deprived of his office as a punishment for the "disparagement" he had allowed her to suffer.

Fairs. Fairs were the only occasions on which unfreemen were allowed to sell staple wares within the Burghs. Fairs had their origin with the assemblages of people met to celebrate the festivals of the Romish Church. The people availed themselves of these occasions to traffic with each other. The clergy exacted fines by way of penance for the offence. These fines glided into regular dues or customs. On the institution of Royal Burghs, certain days were named in their charters, usually saints days, on which strangers under the respective designations of cromars stallangers, dustifoots, on the payment of prescribed dues to the funds of the Burghs, were allowed to trade without restriction. The original word "feria", the latin for a holiday (dies feria) appears under that of "fair". Fairs had some peculiar privileges besides the liberty of trading. A master could not claim his fugitive bondman, nor could any one be arrested for debt in a fair.

Markets. Markets were institutions distinct from fairs. They were appointed to be held once or twice a week. Strangers were allowed to bring perishable commodities, or, as they were sometimes called, "vivers", for sale within Burgh "at market" time "and market place".

Burgesses. The inhabitants of the Burghs were of three classes; Burgesses, to whom were limited the rights of trading, and all municipal officers; Freeholders, holders or proprietors of heritable property. These two classes formed what was called the community. The third was composed of inhabitants who were neither Burgesses nor freeholders. These had no municipal privileges whatever, not even that of residence as a matter of right.

Head Court. Meetings of the community called head courts, to deliberate on the common affairs, were held at Michaelmas, the Nativity and at Easter. At the Michaelmas court, the Magistrates and Councillors were ordained to be chosen, "of faithful men of gude report be the honest men of the Burgh". The disorders that sometimes occurred at these elections were the cause, or afforded the pretext, for depriving the community of the right of election; and the notable device was invented of requiring the Town Councillors under certain restrictions in some Burghs, to elect their successors. Head Courts, however, continued to be held and to control the proceedings of the Council. At the Michaelmas court the newly elected Magistrates appeared and took the oaths of office. These proceedings appeared to be considered a confirmation of their election. The Magistrates were judges in all civil causes, and in all criminal causes except the four pleas of the Crown. In early times they fully exercised their powers. An appeal lay from the Burgh Courts to the King's Chamberlain in a court usually held at Haddington, with assessors appointed by Edinburgh, Stirling, Berwick and Roxburgh; or when the latter two were in hands of the English, by Lanark and Linlithgow, in place of them. This court has for a long time been disused – The court of Session and the circuit court of Justiciary having come in place of it.

The Burgh Reform Act of 1832 has transferred to the owners and occupiers of heritable property of the value of ten pounds and upwards, the right of electing the Town Councillors. The revenues of the Burghs were derived chiefly from the rents of land, a tax called small customs paid for the right of bringing in commodities for sale within the Burgh or for passing through it; and the money paid by Burgesses on their admission. In Burghs having harbours, taxes were exacted from the shipping under the name of anchorage, shore-dues, and other names.

Barons and the great freeholders were exempt from these payments for things for their own property use.

Commissioners to Parliament. Each Royal Burgh sent one or more Commissioners to represent it in Parliament, and in the convention of Boroughs, and, after the Reformation, in the assemblies of the Church, whether provincial or general. The Town Councils could direct their representatives in these bodies how to vote on any occasion. The representatives of the Burghs in the ecclesiastical assemblies were not necessarily office-bearers in the Church for a long time after the Reformation.

Guildry and Trades. Burgesses in most of the Burghs were divided into subordinate incorporations. Of these the Guildry or Merchant Guild was the chief. From its members the Magistrates and the majority of the councillors were ordained to be chosen. They had the exclusive rights of trading. The crafts, or trades as they were called in later times, were composed of those who "wrought with their hands". They were associated together into separate incorporations, according to their different occupations. If any member of the crafts entered the Guild, he was obliged to discontinue manual labour. Admission as a Burgess was a necessary preliminary to admission into any of these incorporations.

Burgesses were also divided into real and honorary. The first were residents bearing scot and lot and watching and warding when required by the Magistrates. The others were merely nominal – the name and rank being conferred on non-residents as a mark of respect and appeared to be valued by persons of condition.

Burghs of Regality and Barony. Besides the Burghs Royal there were Burghs erected by Lords of Regality and Barons, called respectively Burghs of Regality and Baron Burghs and governed by Magistrates appointed by them. The inhabitants of these places had few privileges which the rural inhabitants did not possess and the authority of their Magistrates was limited to petty cases either civil or criminal.

BURGH OF BURNTISLAND

Name. The name of Burntisland is of uncertain derivation. The latter part of the word has been imagined to be derived from the almost insular position of the town, or from the island which forms the south west boundary of the harbour. Amongst the various ways in which the word has been successively written are Byrtland, Byrtiland, Bruntiland, Burntisland. Part of the ground now included in the Royalty was anciently called Ereffland and Cunningarland or rabbit warren. In the several charters of the Burgh the harbour is called "Portus Gratiae" and "Portus Salutis".

But neither these nor any equivalent expression were in common use applied to it.

Town. The harbour and the adjoining territory were the property of the Abbot and Monks of Dunfermline

Abbey; and the town existed as a burgh of Regality under them in the year 1506, but how long before that time I have not been able to discover. The island already referred to and the neighbouring shore formed together a natural harbour and would be resorted to as a place of shelter for ships and a landing place. Being the nearest point on the coast of Fife to Leith, it would early become a ferry station. Houses would be built for seafaring people, and thus a town would arise.

Parish. The parish now called Burntisland anciently formed part of the parish of Kinghorn (or more correctly Kingorne) and was called Little Kingorne or Kingorne Waster; and what is now called Kinghorn was called Great Kingorne or Kingorne Easter. The village now called Kirkton was called the Toun of Kingorne Waster. The church, the Minister's manse, and parish burying ground were there. The church is now in ruins, and is surrounded by the burying ground, which is still used.

Church. It is recorded that the church of Great Kingorne was consecrated by David Andrews, on the 15th and the church of Little Kingorne on the 14th of the Kalends of June 1243 (the 16th and 17th of May respectively).[20]

The whole parish and its two churches were dedicated to Saint Adamnan, successor of Saint Columba in the office of Abbot of Iona.

Royal Burgh. In the year 1541 James the fifth gave certain lands to George, Archdeacon of St. Andrews and Commendator of Dunfermline, in exchange for the harbour of Burntisland and "sax acres" of land adjoining thereto, and erected them into a Burgh Royal. The town was proclaimed as a Burgh Royal with the customary solemnities in the year 1568. But the possession of its privileges seems to have been successfully opposed by the Commendator of Dunfermline. It is indeed uncertain if it ever fully enjoyed them, for in the year 1574 a charter erecting it into a Burgh of Regality, passing over the first Royal charter without notice, was granted by the Commendator, Lord Robert Pitcairn.

New Royal Charter. In the year 1585 a new Royal Charter was obtained substantially the same as that of 1541; but on this occasion confirmed by act of Parliament. This Charter sets forth that King James the sixth having found that his ancestor King James the fifth as a reward for the gratuitous services rendered to him and his predecessors, Kings of Scotland, by the inhabitants of Byrtiland "since" its erection into a great civil community "and to encourage them to go forward in increasing their numbers and in prosecuting trade and navigation, had at great expense constructed the port called the Port of Grace, and disposed [sic] it and the lands adjoining thereto acquired from the Abbots and Monks of Dunfermline to the provost, Bailies, Council and community thereof, and erected these lands into a free Royal Burgh with all the liberties, privileges and immunities granted or to be granted to such institutions "all things non nominate being to be held as nominate as well above the earth as under the earth far off as at hand therefore renews and confirms the said Charter of erection".[21]

Boundaries. The boundaries of the Burgh, as described in both Charters, begin at the west bulwark, now called the half moon, on the west from the point passing under the fortalice of Burntisland, now called Rossend Castle eastward, and then passing to the Broom Hill and going by the weather glow thereof to Greigshole, thence by Craigkennoquhy to the sea, together with the port called the Port of Grace.

The space included in these boundaries is much more than the six acres purchased from the Convent. For what was probably a claim for compensation for the excess, the Earls of Tweeddale, as succeeding to the rights of the abbey, claimed a right to exact a tax called Burgh Mail. Passing over the Royal Charter de novo damus, and acting on the powers conferred by the charter granted by Lord Robert Pitcairn, they claimed a right to review the administration of the Magistrates and to summon the Burgesses to give service in the court of the Regality of Dunfermline. These pretensions of the Tweeddale family were always successfully opposed, but frequently renewed, till towards the end of the seventeenth century, when they were formally abandoned.

About the beginning of that century a more formidable assailant of the rights of the Burgh appeared in the High Chancellor. A proposal or claim was made to have the holding of the town transferred from the King to the Queen. If this had been effected, it appears the inhabitants would have been deprived of their corporate privileges. How this would have been brought about I am unable to explain but it was so clearly understood at the time that the community unanimously resolved to resist it by every means in their power.

These proceedings of the Chancellor were instigated by Sir Robert Melville of Hall Hill and Burntisland castle. Sir Robert found that the whole space between the inner wall of the Castle and the sea was included in the bounds described in the Royal Charter, and he claimed that ground as his private property, and also asserted that the town was adstricted to the Sea Mills which belonged to him. Both these claims were resisted by the community. His influence, however, prevailed so far that the town was deprived for some time of several of its

---

[20] This is correct, as the old Julian calendar counts backwards from the Kalends (or first) of the following month.

[21] The punctuation in this paragraph is incorrect, but is reproduced as it appears in the original.

rights, or at leasi was not allowed fully to exercise them. The Burgh during this time sent no Commissioners to Parliament or the Convention.

Sir Robert Melville, now occasionally called Lord Burntisland and Lord Melville, had been for many years provost of the Burgh, but the community at this time applied to Sir George Home, afterwards Earl of Dunbar, to accept of that office and to protect them by his influence at court against the Melvilles. This he promised to do and was elected Provost accordingly. The Melvilles, however, after a few years regained their influence, and Sir William[22], son of the Robert, was appointed Provost. Never the less the feud still continued, and the Chancellor, as Bailie of the Regality, at his instigation harassed the inhabitants as before.

Charter de novo damus. In 1632 the Town Council applied to the Viscount Stirling for his assistance to procure a new Royal Charter, all swearing "by the extension of the right hand" to keep the matter secret. In 1633 a new Charter was passed at the court at London, and sent on to the keeper of the signet to be sealed. These proceedings having come to the knowledge of Lord Melville he expressed his concurrence in them but desired to see the Charter before it passed the signet. This the Council at first refused, but it appearing that he had sufficient power to prevent the Charter from being sealed, was at last reluctantly granted. On inspecting the Charter he found that as in that of 1585 the part of his property already referred to was within the bounds of the Burgh, and he expressed his resolution to oppose its confirmation unless such alterations were made in it as he required. After many conferences between his Lordship and the leading men of the Burgh, and by the intervention of Mr John Mitchelson, the Minister of the Parish, he consented to withdraw his opposition on the Council making a declaration to the following effect, and inserting it in the Council Books – that the Bounds of the Burgh as described in the new charter interfere in some respects with the heritage of the Lord Melville, and that this was altogether contrary to the intentions of the promoters thereof, therefore and considering the great benefit bestowed on the Burgh by the said Lord and his late father, especially that it was by their influence that the town was erected into a Royal Burgh and that the Kirk at the Kirkton was abandoned and the new Kirk constituted the Parish Kirk, and farther to prevent disputes, declare that the Castle Bank does not belong to the town and that the inhabitants have only a road from the West Bulwark eastward to the house of Orrock of Orrock.

Lord Melville also desired that the Council should acknowledge that the inhabitants were adstricted to the Sea Mills; but this they refused to do.

On the 4th June 1633 the new Charter was sent to Sir John Hay, with three pieces of gold for himself to have it confirmed by Act of Parliament. On the 2nd of July the Act was passed accordingly. At the same time another Act was passed confirming that of James the sixth for granting 500 merks yearly to the Minister of the Parish to be paid from the Exchequer.

These acts were ordered to be put in the "Black Kist and the amorio". The expense of both was "500 merks and 60 Punds".

I have endeavoured to give the substance of the proceedings which issued in the full establishment and recognition of the town as a Royal Burgh. Personal freedom in some considerable respects; the rights of local government; of trading; of holding corporate property; of Parliamentary representation and other rights being involved, sufficiently account for the earnestness with which the community contended for their independence. The Bailie of the Regality of Dunfermline, however, still continued occasionally to assert the subjection of the town to him till towards the end of the century when the Royal Charter being produced in court his claims were finally abandoned.

The grant to the Minister of 500 merks was never regularly paid, and after a few years was altogether withheld. This grant I believe, was in place of a sum paid by the Abbot to the officiating Minister of the parish.

The Magistrates by the Charter referred to were constituted Sheriffs and Water Bailiffs. They were Judges in all civil causes and with the council in criminal cases. But in graver offences a jury of fifteen Burgesses was called and to them the whole matter seemed to be referred. The jury not only found as to the facts, but in the event of conviction assigned the punishment. The punishments were fine, imprisonment, scourging, exposure in the pillory, banishment from the town, and in the case of Burgesses, deprivation of privileges. But the council often proceeded to expel persons from the town without any reason assigned, and these persons not always of humble condition. Sometimes however, they are described as masterless men, unprofitable members, pestiferous persons. The inhabitants were not allowed to sue each other at any but the Burgh Court. Those attempting to do so were fined, imprisoned or banished. Wednesday and Saturday weekly were appointed market days. But the council assumed the right to nominate other days for that purpose.

Fairs and Markets. The feasts of St Peter and St John were appointed fair days. The first is still held on the 29 June old style (10 July). The other had been long discontinued. Besides the trade prosecuted on these

---

[22] Actually Robert, not William.

occasions horse and foot races and other amusements were instituted.

The council consisted of twenty one members including a provost, who was almost always a nobleman or landed gentleman. He was considered the patron of the burgh and was expected to support its interests by his influence. Three bailies, treasurer and procurator fiscal. The other office men were a common clerk, who was some times a Councillor, three constables, Quartermasters to call out the inhabitants to watch and ward or for military service; and two town's officers dressed in the town's livery – that was "four tailed red coats with white lining". There was also a jury of fifteen persons appointed by the Council "to make the statutes", mainly to prescribe at what price Ale, Wine, Meal, Candles and some other things were to be sold. Bread was ordained to be sold at so many ounces for each twelve pennies Scotch. This weight varied from 14 to 17 ounces. This jury also determined how much of each hundred pounds of direct taxes, whether for national or local purposes, each inhabitant had to pay. The business of the Council was conducted with much attention to regularity. Prayers were said at the opening and close of each meeting. Members were required to come in "honest hats and cloaks, and not in bonnets and other unseemly wear". Meetings were held weekly at eight o'clock in the morning. Those absent or departing before the last prayer were fined in twelve shillings scots. All were required "to sit gravely and in silence till their opinion or vote was required by the Moderator". Strict secrecy was required. Those who used profane language were to be fined in thirty shillings; obstinate transgressors were to be expelled the Council. Such were the rules, but the records show that they were but indifferently obeyed.

Burgesses and Freemen paid on their admission from ten merks to thirty pounds scots each, according to their supposed ability, and gave a banquet to the council sometimes called "the spice and wine". The banquet seemed never to be omitted. Freemen's eldest sons were admitted gratis, always excepting the banquet. The new Burgess afterwards appeared in the Burgh court and swore to be faithful to the king; to defend the liberties of the Burgh; and to assist the Magistrates in the due execution of their duty. He required to be of good moral character; of the "true religion", able to bear the king's fine; to reside bear scot and lot, and watch and ward when required; and be owner of a rood of bigget land. Non-residents were held to be honorary only, though their names appeared in the list of Burgesses.

Burgesses were originally all of one rank; but about the beginning the seventeenth century the members of each particular occupation began to associate for the purpose of preventing unfreemen from working within the Burgh, and for preventing strangers from bringing in commodities for sale. The members of each craft contributed to a common fund called a box or mortification for bearing the expense of prosecuting such intruders before the Magistrates. These Associations obtained the sanction of the council on condition that each craft would undertake to support its own poor.

Trades. They were authorised to compel all resident workmen to contribute to their funds. The crafts desired to be incorporated, but the council refusing to make any further concession, they raised an action in the Court of Session to compel the Council to grant their desire. After a protracted litigation the crafts were successful, and each craft obtained a subordinate Charter or, as it was called, a seal of cause, with the usual privileges. These crafts were the Wrights, Masons, Baxters, Tailors, Weavers, Shoemakers and Fleshers. The sailors or Prime-guild[23], Hirers and Maltmen, had each a common fund, but were not incorporated. The Prime-guild still remains and is possessed of considerable property, the proceeds of which are paid to aged members and widows. The others are extinct.

Guildry. The Guildry was the principal incorporation. It began in the year 1616[24] with a society of traders in materials for men and women's clothes, or what was called "merchant goods". These traders claimed an exclusive right to "pack and peel" within Burgh, a right which was not allowed them at that time. At intervals they renewed this claim but unsuccessfully till 1710, when they were fully incorporated with the exclusive right of trading.

Council. Disputes having arisen as to the manner of electing the Council, the whole matter was in 1732 referred to arbitration. By the decreet issued on that occasion the council was to consist, as before, of twenty one persons, of whom fourteen, including all the Magistrates, were to be guild brethren, and seven craftsmen, one of each craft. A Dean of Guild was also appointed with six assessors. Each craft chose its own Deacon, but he had no place in the Council. All the other office-bearers were chosen by the Council. The old council chose the new. The community had no direct voice in the matter. I have endeavoured to describe the condition of the Burgh as it existed, with some unimportant alterations, for a long period. The municipal constitution of Burntisland was substantially the same as that of the other Burghs of Scotland during that time. The internal government of these places was in many respects very defective, and led to great abuses. As a whole, however the existence of these incorporations was conducive to the maintenance of civil and religious liberty during the

---

[23] This is a reference to the Prime Gilt Society.

[24] The year 1606 is given in the 1835 Report of the Royal Commission on Municipal Corporations in Scotland.

tumults of the seventeenth century. The privileges of the Burgesses gave them a greater degree of influence in national affairs than was possessed by the corresponding class of landward people. The Burgesses of Burntisland were generally zealous covenanters, and scarcely less intolerant in principle than was the faction by which they were often oppressed. Succeeding generations owed much of the religious and civil liberty they enjoyed to the covenanters, in spite of what we now see to have been defective in their protestantism. He must indeed have a cold heart that can look otherwise than with admiration on their zeal, and with sympathy on their sufferings in the cause of what they believed to be truth.

After the union with England, the elective franchise for the Burghs was vested in the Town Councils, and was a chief cause why the Burgh system was maintained entire long after its defects were seen and acknowledged by all parties. The smallest modification thereof was obstinately resisted, lest any modification of the British Parliament should thereby be effected. It therefore remained entire till it was entirely removed by the passing of the Burgh Reform Act of 1833.

By this Act the Burgesses were deprived of their peculiar privileges, and their interest in the corporate property was transferred to others. Thus for the public benefit they were virtually extinguished as a class, for the word Burgess in now only an empty name. This act has been followed by many beneficial consequences. The station, however, of Burgh Magistrates has since that time declined.

At Burntisland the public peace was maintained by the ordinary constables. These were composed of Burgess households and young men of respectable station. They exercised a moral authority in the discharge of their duty which we shall look for in vain in a paid police force.

Harbour. About the year 1600 the Harbour appears to have been a slip at the south east corner of the Harbour called the Grey Sunday, for the use of the ferry boats; a pier, or bulwark as it was called, at the north west corner near what is now called the Half Moon, constructed wholly or mostly of wood, and adapted for the reception of the larger class of ships; some kind of work at the Earne Craig (not Iron Craig nor Herring Craig, as it is sometimes called), and probably other piers along the shore.

It has been said, on what authority I know not, that the piers were built and the streets paved by Cromwell; and that the town capitulated to him on condition that he would complete these works. Except that a portion of small amount of the national taxes payable by the town were allowed to be applied to the repair of the Harbour, with a small grant from the exchequer, there is no appearance in the Burgh records of anything having been done during the time of the Commonwealth for these purposes. With these exceptions the Harbour was repaired, the works thereof extended, and the streets paved at the expense of the inhabitants, or by their personal labour, assisted in respect of the Harbour by grants from the Convention, and by contributions from several of the Burghs.

The causeway joining the island to the shore was made in the year 16 [25]. The east head was built about 1620. It was made parallel to the Grey Sunday, apparently for the purpose of sheltering the landing place from the south east wind. The West Head was finished in 1656. These were the only considerable improvements effected on the Harbour works for 150 years after.

They were very imperfectly executed, and stood in constant need of repair, forming – as the Council expressed it in their application to the Government and the Conventions for assistance – "an intolerable burden on the town".

Streets. At the end of the sixteenth century houses had been built along the east side of the Harbour and in a continuous line on both sides of the King High Street as far as the East Port. Parallel to this street was the Back Gate on the south, but the houses do not seem to have been continuous. Farther south was the South Hill having detached houses with gardens. The Kirk Wynd is referred to, and the North Vennel leading to the Kirkton. There were also narrow lanes passing between some of the streets called "Throughs". Between the north side of the High Street and the Broom Hill were gardens, malt kilns, and brew houses. In the middle of the seventeenth century the High Street was partly paved, with a gutter on each side, and the Back Street, with a gutter in the middle. These works had been very imperfectly executed, and were not completed till the end of that century. The gutters were partly of wood. From the frequent orders issued to clear the streets of red and middings, and to make trenches to allow the water to run off, it may be inferred that the streets were in a very bad condition.

Port. At the east end of the High Street an arch was built across the street in 1635, and called the East Port. It was taken down in 1825 [26] by order of the Road Trustees, for the purpose of widening the entrance. Though this erection had no pretensions to architectural beauty, it gave the town a venerable appearance to those entering it from the east, and formed a shelter from the easterly winds. The Trustees promised to erect a

---

[25] The year was omitted, but is likely to have been in the period 1600 to 1620.
[26] The East Port was almost certainly removed in 1843.

handsome structure in place of it. The two square pillars built there shew what was these gentlemen's idea of handsomeness. The South Port and the North Port are referred to in the record, but at what particular point these were I have not discovered. If there were any buildings connected with them, they have long since disappeared.

Forts. During the civil wars of the seventeenth century there were earthern and wooden works constructed for the defence of the town along the Broom Hill, and stone batteries at the south side of the Harbour, called "forths", all mounted with great guns.

Church. The Church, now the Parish Church, is probably the oldest building of the town. The external fabric was built at the expense of the inhabitants, and was completed some short time before 1595. There is a tradition that it was built after the pattern of a church in Holland. The frequent intercourse with that country at this time renders the truth of that tradition not improbable.[27] The seating of the floor of the church was done from time to time by private persons for their own accommodation, by permission of the Council and the Kirk Session.

The Galleries were erected in the year 1613. The greater part of these belongs to the Prime Guild[28] Society. The Guildry, Hammermen, Tailors, Bakers, Maltsmen, and Schoolmaster, have the rest. On the front of the Galleries the insignia of these trades were painted. On the sides of the pillars opposite were texts of scripture intended to apply to the occupations of the several trades. On the other side of the pillars were inscribed the ten commandments and Lord's Prayer, with other portions of Scripture, and the apostles' Creed. Quaint representations of men with sextants and antique ships on the front of the Sailor's loft, were objects of curiosity. The Merchants had their inexplicable figure 4. These have all been obliterated. Their disappearance was very generally regretted. A tower rises from the middle of the church, supported by four massive pillars with arches passing between them, and abutting arches stretching diagonally from each corner. The tower was surmounted by a wooden belfry till 1745, which was then taken down and replaced by the present stone building. It is said that it was intended to carry it to a greater height, but that it was feared that the pillars could not sustain the weight. The pulpit was erected in 1606, and was ordered to be made like the pulpit in Trinity Church in Edinburgh.

On the pillars four ponderous oak beams were laid horizontally. From these to support the roof were many undressed fir posts. The roof was unceiled. The part of the church now occupied by the Communion table seats was occupied with moveable seats and chairs used by the Burghers' wives and families, the men sitting apart in the seats appropriated to their several crafts. A claim having been made by the landward heritors to have space allotted to them whereon to construct seats for themselves, after a long continued dispute it was settled by arbitration that a certain space under the galleries on the north and east sides of the church should belong to them.

The seats then erected had canopies with tawdry carved and gilt ornaments. These canopies were removed for preservation while the repairs of the church were in progress in 1822, the patrician landholders objecting to sit with nothing between their heads and the footboards of the plebeian mechanics. These dignified ornaments disappeared during the repairing of the church. The Magistrates' seat was the only seat retained in its integrity.

For many years after the church had been built and partly furnished, the landward heritors opposed its being constituted the Parish Church, and refused to pay Minister's stipend unless he officiated at the Old Kirk at the Kirkton. After long litigation before the church courts and the Lords Modificators, it was in 1632 constituted the Parish Church. To supplement the Minister's stipend the Burgh contributed sums varying from 200 to 400 merks yearly. It settled down at the latter sum, at which it still remains. This was originally raised by assessment on the inhabitants, along with the other taxes for national and local purposes. But during the civil wars of the seventeenth century, it being found impossible to levy the whole of the taxes demanded from the inhabitants for these purposes, the corporate revenue was drawn on to make up the deficiency of the Minister's and Schoolmaster's stipends.

In this manner these payments glided into permanent charges on the Burgh revenue. Till the year 1656 the Minister's Manse was at the Kirkton, but being found insufficient, the Minister received £20 from the town and £40 from the heritors, in place of a Manse. This agreement was continued till a late period. There is now a suitable Manse at the east end of the Burgh.

The earliest reference to a School in the Burgh records is in the year 1600. In the year 1607 there was a Schoolmaster and an assistant, or, as the latter was called, a School Doctor.

In 1612, the Presbytery, in compliance with an ordinance of the Archbishop of St Andrews, ordered the Council to establish a Grammar School within the Burgh. The Council set forth that they "think it not meet to

---

[27] Current thinking is that Burntisland Parish Church is not modelled on a Dutch church; it is more likely to be unique.

[28] Gilt.

comply therewith", but resolve to have an ordinary School, and to look out for a fit person to be master. It appears that the then incumbent was not considered fit. They afterwards, however, found that as he taught "Inglis" that he was fit, and rented a school house for his accommodation. In 1620, six roods of land were bought at the South Hill, whereon a school-house and dwelling houses for the Master and Doctor were erected.

On this occasion was introduced a custom, continued for many years, of the Master and Doctor delivering the keys of the school-house and of their dwelling houses to the Council in acknowledgement that they held their offices during the pleasure of the Council.

The keys were regularly returned with an admonition to be "more diligent than heretofore". No private schools were allowed except those of women, and they were allowed to teach "lasses and very young boys". In 1635 the salary of the Schoolmaster was 100 merks, afterwards increased to 150. The quarterly fees were, for Latin 12 shillings, for English 9 shillings, of which two thirds belonged to the Master and one third to the Doctor. I see no mention of a salary to the Doctor, but he was usually reader of prayers and precentor in the church, for which he had an allowance. In 1656 a woman teacher had a free house, and in 1743 Two pounds sterling were given on condition that she taught two or three scholars free. In 1803 the old school house was taken down, and a new building erected at the east end of the Broom Hill for school and Master's houses, a shapeless erection, but well aired.

Till the beginning of the seventeenth century the meetings of the Council were held in "the Clerk's Chamber". A house was hired for a prison.

In the year 1613 a tollbooth or town-house was begun to be built, and was finished in 1620. It stood at the opening of the High Street near the Harbour. It was a heavy looking building with a tower, belfry, and clock on the east gable.

On the first floor of the tower were wretched cells for criminal prisoners, and two small rooms above for debtors – places in which no human being could long retain health of either mind or body. A large hall and a court and council room occupied the west part of the building. This building was taken down in 1843 and a neat though small town house erected in the High Street at the corner of the Kirk Wynd. On the ground occupied by the new town house were the shambles, and in early times a place for the sale of county produce. The cross was about the middle of the High Street, at which there was some kind of wooden fabric and the pillar at which offenders were exposed.

In 1736 a church was built on the south side of the High Street by those who had shortly before seceded from the Established Church[29]. It was a heavy and unornamented building, but has of late been much improved both internally and externally, and is now a commodious and respectable place of worship.

The Free Church, built at the sole expense of Mr John Young of Colinswell and of his brother, Robert Young, is situated close to the Parish Church; but being found too small for the congregation, a site has been acquired on the south side of the High Street, near the East Port, for a new church.

Besides the ground on which the town is built, the Royalty includes the Links, the Broom Hills, and the Lammerlaws. The Burgesses have the privilege of using the Links for grazing cattle. It is also used as a place of exercise, for playing golf and other games. It is of very great value to the inhabitants and with the Broom Hills and Criagkennoquhy, is secured in perpetuity to them as a place of recreation. In 1810 the Magistrates feued part of the Links. The inhabitants opposed this proceeding and an interdict was obtained from the Court of Session which has become perpetual. The Railway Company have acquired a part of the Links at the south east corner by authority of Parliament, on which they have erected workshops.

From the year 1600 and probably before, till near the end of last century, the number of the inhabitants seemed to vary very little. In that year and till the time I have stated, there were about 250 names on the stent roll. These were all either heritors or house holders. Allowing 50 more for those unable to pay any direct tax, this would give about 1200 as the number of the inhabitants. The importance of Burntisland, compared with that of other Burghs, may be roughly calculated by the part of each £100 of direct taxes each town had to pay, and by the number of men appointed to be levied from each for military service. In 1670 Burntisland paid £1"3/- of each £100; Edinburgh paid £33"6"8; Glasgow £31"; Aberdeen £7; Perth £3"17/-; Cupar £1; Dysart ad Dunfermline £ -"16/- each; Kinghorn £ -"9/-; Inverkeithing £-"8/-; and the rest in various sums down to one shilling, as in the case of Inverbervie and North Berwick.

In 1645, of 1879 men appointed to be levied by the Burghs for military service, 16 were assigned to Burntisland; 574 to Edinburgh; to Cupar 24; to Dunfermline 12; Dysart 31; Kinghorn 14; Kirkcaldy 46; St Andrews 30.

These ways of judging gave different results; the first is founded on wealth, and the second on population.

Till about the middle of the last century the communication with the county was by roads fit to be used by

---

[29] The Secession in Burntisland took place in 1738, and the Seceders' new church building was erected in 1743.

persons travelling on foot or on horseback. The required width was no more than sufficient to allow two horses carrying creels to pass each other. The road to the north passed by the Kirkton, Grange and Dunearn to Kinross; to the west in front of Geds Mill by where Colinswell house now stands to Aberdour; to the east, through the Links, Lochies and Bents by the defile at the east end of these, by Kinghorn Loch to Kirkcaldy.

These lines of road have been several times altered within the last hundred years.

From the earliest records it appears that the principal inhabitants were seafaring people, navigating their own vessels in foreign and coasting voyages. In 1640 there were nine vessels belonging to the town of 50 tons burthen and upwards namely one of 50 tons, one of 80 tons, one of 85 tons, one of 105 tons, two of 115 tons, one of 120 tons and one of 160 tons. Besides these there were smaller vessels called crears, employed as coasters. There were also ferry boats, of which some were decked and some open boats, but the exact number I have not seen stated. The providing of accommodation for travellers by the Ferry to and from Leith gave employment to many persons, almost every house appeared to be a regular or occasional place of lodging for travellers. Many were employed in navigating the Ferry Boats, and many in providing horses for travellers. These horses were accompanied on their journeys by men on foot. In 1689 the number of brewers was 43, of Vintners 9.

The craftsmen were employed in making commodities for the use of the inhabitants of the town and neighbourhood. They seem, however, to have had little skill in their trades, for it required all their vigilance to prevent the workmen of the neighbouring towns from intruding on them. The Weavers, Tailors and Butchers of Aberdour were a sore cause of annoyance. When any important piece of work was to be done, workmen were brought from Dundee, Dunfermline, and other places to execute it.

The foreign trade of the town was comparatively extensive. It consisted chiefly of importing wood from Norway; flax from Flanders; wine from France; malt and grain from England. Beef, hides and grain were brought from the north of Scotland. A great part of these things were for merchants of Dunfermline, Cupar, Dundee and other places. There was a considerable trade in the exportation of coals to Holland and Flanders. These were brought on horseback from Fordell and other collieries.

Rossend Castle. The Castle of Burntisland now called Rossend Castle, is the only ancient building in the immediate neighbourhood of Burntisland.

Its early name was the "Tower of Kinghorn Waster" to distinguish it from Glammis Tower or the "Tower of Kinghorne Easter". The exact time of its erection I believe, cannot now be ascertained. It was probably a Keep or place of refuge in troublous times. The earliest accounts of it set forth that Durie of that Ilk, Abbot of Dunfermline, built the north and south wings in the year 1382. The armorial bearings of the Duries are inserted in the wall over the principal door. So many of that family were successively Abbots that the house was sometimes called Abbots Hall. In the Chartulary of Dunfermline Abbey there is recorded a grant of the lands of Nether Grange and Kinghorne Waster together with the keep or fort of the same, and the lands of Erefland and Cunningarland, now Burntisland. This grant is dated 1538. It is probable that though the Duries had long been in the actual possession of these places, they had then for the first time acquired them as private property. At the Reformation the Duries were dispossessed of these lands, and they were bestowed on Sir William Kirkcaldy of Grange so honourably distinguished as a soldier for his adherence to the Reformation, and for his attachment to the unhappy Queen Mary. On his death by the hands of the public executioner, these lands appear to have been transferred to the Melvilles of Hall Hill, ancestors of the Earls of Leven and Melville.

St Margaret, wife of Malcolm Canmore, had been buried at Dunfermline. Her remains were collected by King Alexander the III, and the bones placed in a silver chest which at the Reformation was sent to the Castle of Edinburgh and afterwards removed to that of Burntisland by Father Durie.

Queen Mary in her journeys through Fife often lodged here. The apartment which she occupied on these occasions is a wainscoted room in the old square tower and two closets cut out in the wall, which is here ten feet thick. In one of these closets is the entrance to a stair said to have led down to the seashore. The room referred to goes by the name of the State bedchamber.

During the civil wars of the seventeenth century this place was held by the covenanters, and was the headquarters of their forces in the neighbourhood. The town and castle were besieged by the army of the Commonwealth, and surrendered on 10th April 1651[30] on condition, it is said, that the victims would be at the expense of repairing the harbour and paving the streets: conditions, if they ever existed, certainly never fulfilled.

On 22 July of that year Cromwell was at Burntisland, and from that place addressed a letter to the Speaker of the House of Commons, commending the place as "pretty strong, but marvellously capable of improvement without great charge, the harbour being at springtides a fathom deeper than that of Leith". He states that he took

---

[30] The correct date is almost certainly 27 July 1651.

two or three small msn-of-war [sic] with thirty or forty guns. The Castle became the property of the Earls of Melville and afterwards of the Earls of Wemyss and Elgin. Sir James Wemyss of Bogie was in 1672 created Lord Burntisland, and had a seat in the Scottish Parliament until his death in 1687.

BURGH RECORDS

1596. The records of the Burgh begin this year. Sir Robert Melville, proprietor of the Castle, was Provost. There was no regular Minister of the parish. Mr William Scott officiated, and was paid 200 merks yearly, raised by assessment on the inhabitants. There was a reader of public prayers who was also Schoolmaster, but for whom there was no settled provision. For his support, the Council nominated certain of the "honestest men" of the town to lodge him in their houses by turns. The trade of the town seemed considerable, consisting of importations for merchants in Dunfermline, Aberdour, Leith and Edinburgh.

1597. Common Seal. A Common Seal was adopted, having on it the figure of King James V in full armour, no doubt as an expression of gratitude for having conferred on the town the status of a Burgh Royal. At this time the Burgh sent two Commissioners to Parliament and one to the Convention of Boroughs.

Reductions. The attempt already referred to reduce the town to the state of Burgh of Regality to hold off the Commendator of Dunfermline, was made. To bear the expense of resisting this measure, the inhabitants were assessed at thirteen shillings and four pennies on each rood of land.

1598. Robert Brown accused Janet Allan of having caused the death of his son by witchcraft. The Magistrates refused to interfere unless security were given that they would be relieved of the expense of trying and of executing her, if found guilty. The required security being given, Janet was tried by a jury of fifteen persons, found guilty, and sentenced to be "burnt quick". The sentence, however was not executed, for what cause is not recorded, for soon after she was again accused of a similar crime, and again sentenced to be burnt. But whether at last poor Janet was actually murdered does not appear.

Witchcraft. A letter was received from Sir Robert Melville on behalf of the Government, ordering strict account to be taken of all persons suspected of witchcraft.

A Riotous Councillor. There were many disorders committed in the town at this time, for instance, a Town Councillor abused the Bailies in the Council house, and on being ordered to go to ward, refused to surrender, drew his whanger, threw down his glove, and challenged them to single combat, and then betook himself to his own house from the "windock" of which he continued the wordy warfare. For all which offences he was brought before a Head court, fined in ten merks, ordained to behave well in future, and to ask pardon of the Council on his knees in the church, after the Wednesday preaching.

Purgation. the council ordered the town to be "purged of slanderous, suspicious and unprofitable members", which was done.

Grant of 500 merks and Modificators' refusal. The grant of 500 merks yearly for the Minister's stipend was procured this year from the King; but the Lords of Modificators refused to ratify it; where upon a Commissioner was sent to the President to obtain his consent; and as it was believed that he bore a grudge against certain individuals in the town, the commissioner was authorized to promise that these persons should be banished, if that would content him.

Auld and New Kirks. The fabric of the New Kirk was completed at this time, a bell put in the steeple, and public worship celebrated there, but the landward heritors refusing to pay their part of the Minister's stipend unless he preached at the Old Kirk at the Kirkton, Mr William Simpson, who had been duly appointed Minister craved leave of the Council to be allowed to officiate there; and further desired them if they would not allow this, to obtain another Minister "that can live on his ain, for there is no remeid for him but to pass to the Auld Kirk or want his stipend". On this representation the Council applied to the King and Privy Council to have the Minister interdicted from preaching at the Auld Kirk, and to compel the landward people to absent themselves from it.

School. The Council declared that no person shall be allowed to set up a school without their leave.

Arming. The inhabitants of the town ordered to provide themselves either with corslet, head piece, sword and pike; or with a musket, staff, head piece and sword.

General Assembly and Council. A meeting of the General Assembly of the Church was held at Burntisland on the 10th March 1601, at which the King was present. The only notice of this meeting in the Council Record is the following:-

"Apud Burntisland tertio Mch. 1601. The Baillies and Council quhais names follow, viz x x x being convenit togidder in counsall ordains an convenient house to be providit for ye convention of ye ministerie with His Majesty and his commissioners to be halden wt-in y^ce burgh on the tent day of Mch instant and ordains cules to be providit to serve for fyre for ye said house, during the time of the said convention; and all in ane voice thinks Mr Andro Wilson his lodging most convenient for y^t purpose and requires him to spare ye same to that effect."

The Mr Andro Wilson referred to was common clerk, and his lodging was at the South Hill. This house would probably be for lodging the members. The meetings of the Assembly would likely be held in the new Kirk.

Freight at the Ferry and the Melvilles. Sir Robert Melville complained that his servants had been overcharged by the Ferriers (Ferry boatmen) for freight. In order to propitiate him the Council ordered the rates to be paid for his servants to be 12d for each footman; three shillings & 4d for each man and horse; 26 shillings and 8 pennies for a boat. To what extent Sir Robert was favoured is not said. In 1621 the freight for each person was 2 shillings, and for a boat 40 shillings.

Auld and New Kirks. The Minister having left the charge, the Council, which seems to have assumed the power of providing a minister for the Parish, by advice of the Presbytery desired "Mr William Watson to tak the pains to teach at the Kirk on Sunday", to the effect that the people may give their assent to his admission. After proceedings before the several Church Courts, the Assembly ordained him to be settled at Burntisland, the Magistrates agreeing to give him two hundred pounds yearly. The Presbytery, however, refused to acknowledge the New Kirk, and wished to "plant" him at the Auld Kirk. This the council refused to allow.

It appears that he afterwards officiated at the New Kirk, on what conditions is not said.

William Watson Minister. This Mr William Watson was one of the four ministers who some years afterwards were called up to London by order of the King, to keep them out of the way till his intended innovations in church government were completed.

1602. Church Seating. An assessment of 400 pounds was levied on the inhabitants to bear the expense of seating the church, including a pulpit to be made like that of the Trinity Church in Edinburgh.

Rioting, and Duries of Grange. A complaint was made to the King against John Durie (of Grange, I presume) and his brother, of wrong done to John Baxter, Burgess, with baton, dagger, and sword, and craving redress. The Duries had been convicted of the offence by the Magistrates, but refused to submit to them, upon which James and John Boswell, sons of the laird of Balmuto, proposed to refer the matter to arbitration. The Bailies and Council asserted it to be against the "common voice, honour and liberties of the Burgh to refer the question to any judges but themselves; and if the Duries shall still refuse to submit themselves, resolve to persevere in their application to the King." This affair remained unsettled till August 1604, when the minister, Mr William Watson, already referred to, informed the Council that unless they were reconciled to the Duries, and that without the Duries acknowledging themselves in the wrong, he would not dispense the Communion. The Council informed him that they were bound by their own acts to exact a confession from the Duries, but for the sake of peace, agreed to refer the matter to "the said Mr William himself". Here is a notable instance of inconsistency. This Mr Watson was no obscure person, but on the contrary, as already noticed, a leader of the strictest sect of the Presbyterians; yet does he make the dispensation of the most solemn ordinance of religion depend upon the official conduct of the Burgh Magistrates.

Slander. Gill Watson was convicted by the Council of "calling the pastor a Devil", and ordained to stand at the cross with a paper on her head with an inscription in large letters setting forth her offence; and to stand with the same ornament at the north east pillar of the Kirk during the forenoon preaching.

Schoolmaster and School Doctor. A Schoolmaster and School Doctor were regularly appointed this year; the latter was to be "taker up of the psalm, keeper of the Kirk records, and reader of prayers in the Kirk".

Ferry. The city of Edinburgh attempted to levy a tax of twelve pennies on each ferry boat for every time it crossed the Ferry. This imposition was resisted by Burntisland and Kinghorn successfully.

Plague. The plague prevailed this year in Edinburgh, Leith, Kinghorn, Perth, and in the neighbourhood. The town was strictly watched day and night, to prevent persons from these places from entering it. Many of the inhabitants were suspected of being infected and therefore "enclosed" – that is, shut up in their houses. When this was resorted to they were not allowed to come out again without leave from the Council. Inspectors were appointed to examine the suspected, and on their report depended the treatment they experienced. The breaking out of boils on the body was considered a symptom of the disease. As soon as a suspicion of its approach arose, all dogs, cats and swine were ordered to be killed, in the belief apparently that these animals propagated the infection. The streets were ordered to be cleared of "Middings, red and refuse", and paved gutters were ordered to be made to carry off the standing water. At this time, recruits for the King of Sweden were lodged in the town preparatory to embarkation. These, with all poor persons and beggars, were ordered to be expelled. The inhabitants continued for several years after this to live in a constant state of alarm about the plague. Much of the time of the council seemed to be occupied in making regulations for protection against the infection. In spite, however, of all their precautions, the town had a severe visitation of the disease in 1608. On the 27th August, it having been discovered that three or four persons had died of the "sickness", the Council ordered that "cleangers" be sought for from Kinghorn to "tack order with this sickness", and to bury those who had died of it. The Council ordered that the inhabitants were not to hold intercourse with each other. Twenty pounds were paid to the workmen for graves. Two loads of white bread were received as a gift from the inhabitants of Kirkcaldy, for the poor; and thirty pounds were taken from "the Tuesdays box" for their support. Poor persons, when attacked, were taken from their own houses to "lodges" on the south side of the Links. If they appeared to be recovering, they were removed to lodges on the north side, and there remained till free from the disease. But nothing belonging to them was permitted to be brought into the town. Some kind of kilns were built and cauldrons for cleansing the "foul gear" were provided. The cleansers were a disorderly set. They extracted four pounds from the friends of deceased persons for attendance, above the regular allowance, and also abstracted goods in place of money.

An agreement was therefore made with them that they were to have one hundred pounds and their maintenance, till the town was cleansed. It appears that the Magistrates lost almost all authority during this visitation. Crimes and offences of various kinds prevailed to an unusual extent. As some remedy for this state of matters; fourteen persons were appointed with the power of Bailies, and twenty eight assessors. These were ordered to call out the inhabitants to watch by turns.

None were allowed to leave the town lest this duty should be evaded; nor were any allowed to enter it without leave, I presume. The town was in a state of siege, all the neighbouring places having interdicted intercourse with it. On the 28th November the town was considered free from the disease; and those who lodged in the Links were allowed to come in, but not to go at large till trial was made of the state of their health. The "cleangers" were conveyed to Kinghorn and delivered to the authorities there at the "West Port thereof". I have no where seen it recorded how many died on this occasion, but it must have been considerable – chiefly poor persons.

Religious Observance. Immediately after the town was considered free from the plague, the Council set about enforcing attendance on religious ordinances, apparently as an expression of their gratitude to God for the deliverance. All persons were enjoined to attend the service of the church on Sundays and other days, especially they required that the Tuesday's preaching be better attended, and the Sabbath better kept. They therefore ordained that all persons absent from the church on Sabbath shall be warded in the Tron House for twelve hours, "without meat or drink but bread and water", or pay a fine of twenty shillings for the first offence, thirty for the second, forty for the third, all without prejudice to the censure of the Kirk Session. They also ordained that the whole inhabitants, "as well man as wife" should be present at the Tuesday's preaching, and that the "hail booth doors shall be closed at the ringing of the third bell, under the pain of forty pennies in law toties quoties as often as they failyie". I have thus endeavoured to give an account of the visitation of the "sickness", from its appearance in the town in 1602, to its disappearance in 1608.

Minister sent to London. In 1606, the minister, Mr William Watson, and other ministers, were called up to London by the King, under the pretence of taking their opinion on the state of ecclesiastical affairs, but in reality to prevent them from opposing the intended innovations in church government. The Council appointed certain "honest men" to provide a horse to carry the said Mr William to London, and nominated one of the Bailies to accompany him part of the way. The Bailie on his return reported that he had conveyed him a space beyond Berwick.

Convention of Burghs. On the 22nd November a meeting of the convention of burghs was held at Burntisland. "Ale with some wastle and shortbread" was provided for the members. The Councillors were ordered to receive them in their "best array". Nothing else is recorded anent it.

Earl of Dunbar and Sir Robert Melville. Thirlage, The Earl of Dunbar was again elected Provost, and promised to do his best to defeat the renewed attempts of Sir Robert Melville and his Lady, Lady Ross, to get the town disfranchised. The cause of this new attempt on the liberties of the Burgh was the continued opposition of the inhabitants to the thirlage of the Sea Mills. On this occasion, in order to propitiate Sir Robert and his Lady, the Council resolved "to treat them with courtesy and wait on them on Sundays at the Castle gate, and accompany them to the Kirk". The Bishop of Brechin (Lamb?) was mediator on this occasion; but neither the courtesy of the Council nor the mediation of the Bishop had the desired effect.

Stipend. On the return of the minister from London the old grant of 500 merks toward his stipend was renewed by the government; but the assessment for stipend on the inhabitants was continued.

Quarrel anent Poor's Money. A quarrel having arisen between the Magistrates and the Kirk Session as to which of them had the right to distribute the Kirk collections for the poor, the Council sent Commissioners to the minister to treat about the matter. The commissioners reported that the minister had "used sundry injurious and blasphemous words nought worthy to be repeated". The Council applied to the Bishop of St Andrews for redress, but if the Bishop did anything in the matter it is not recorded.

1610. Anchorage. The owners of ships using the harbour were ordered to pay six shillings and eight pence each, without distinction of size, before delivering their cargo. This is the origin of the duty called anchorage. It was afterwards charged according to the tonnage of the vessels.

1612. Schoolmaster. The Presbytery of Kirkcaldy in compliance with an ordinance of the Archbishop of

St Andrews, desired the council to establish a Grammar School, and to get some scholar to be master thereof. At first the Council agreed by plurality of votes to comply, but afterwards refused on the ground that they had no funds to bear the expense; and that they could not dismiss David Adamson, who taught "Inglis" and read the prayers for the stipend the Master was wont to receive. They also intimated to the Presbytery that if they wished David Adamson to be deposed, they must do it themselves.

In the year 1620, a regular and qualified schoolmaster was appointed with a salary of 100 merks, 50 of which were paid by the "Kirk Session, and 50 by the Prime Guild[31]. Twelve shillings were paid quarterly by each scholar, of which two thirds were for the Master and one third for the Doctor. The salary was afterwards increased to 150 merks, and a house for a school house rented at eight pounds yearly. Six roods of land were bought at the south hill on which to build a school house and dwelling house for the Master and Doctor. These buildings were erected accordingly. The expense of the mason work is given at sixty six pounds and £34"13"4 for wright work. They remained till the beginning of this century. The place near which they stood still goes under the name of the "Scholars' Brae".

Crime. Crimes and offences greatly prevailed in the town about this time. They are described as bloodwits, turbulances, profane swearing, opposing the Magistrates, abusing the minister, and also some unnamable crimes. It seemed as if society had fallen into barbarism.

Murder. John brown and his son, sailors belonging to Burntisland, were hanged at Leith or Edinburgh, for throwing three Spanish merchants into the sea. Their heads were sent over and put up on posts at the Island.

Prisoners. The expense of supporting prisoners was ordered by the Magistrates to be borne by the parties at whose instance they were incarcerated.

Thirteen pennies daily was the prescribed allowance (1½d sterling).

Privileges and Reduction. This year a regular action at the instigation of Sir Robert Melville and his wife was brought by the Chancellor of the Abbey of Dunfermline for payment of Burgh mail; and afterwards another action for depriving the town of all its privileges. The minister and principal inhabitants endeavoured, but in vain, to get the Chancellor to restrict the action to having the town reduced from Burgh Royal to a Burgh of Regality. Some kind of compromise, however, appears to have been afterwards made. I have not been able to discover how it was brought about, there being a blank of two years in the record. In the year 1617 the town was nominally in the possession of its municipal privileges, but really in a state of vassalage to Sir Robert Melville, now called Lord Burntisland, and the Earl of Dunfermline. The former was again Provost.

New Charter. The Council and chief inhabitants resolved secretly to apply to the King for a new charter.

Manse. The bishop and synodal Assembly resolved to build a manse for the minister at the Kirkton. This measure was strongly resisted by the Council.

1624. Plague. The plague prevailing at this time in Leith, Edinburgh and some foreign places, the town was strictly watched to prevent any "but honest famous persons" from entering it; all "unco beggars" were expelled, and the equipages (crews) of ships examined as to the state of their health before allowing them to land.

Levies of Seamen. The Privy Council ordered the Magistrates to provide pilots and seamen to carry His Majesty's ship "Assurance" to the Thames. The Council reported that there were no pilots of sufficient skill here, and that all the sailors had fled for fear of the press.

The Magistrates were subsequently ordered to report how many ships belonged to the town; of what size and how equipped. The Privy Council then first ordered ten men to be levied, and afterwards eight, to man His Majesty's fleet. The Magistrates were afterwards ordered to put in ward all idle and masterless men wanting the means of subsistence, till a captain was sent to take charge of them. This order was not complied with.

Militia. Each Burgess was ordered by the Town Council to provide himself with weapons according to his estate. Such of the inhabitants fit to bear arms were afterwards embodied under the name of militia. There were two companies, one of married and one of unmarried men. Each had a stand of colours with an ensign to carry them; a commander and sergeants "to keep the men in the ranks at the weapon shawings".

Soldiers. A company of King,s soldiers under Colonal Mackay were quartered in the town at this time. They were very disorderly, refused to pay for the ale and beer they drank, and gave "bluidy strokes to many". The Council petitioned the Privy Council that they be expelled, and in the meantime disarmed.

Recruiting. The Magistrates were required by the Earl of Morton to inform him how many men they could send to go with him to the Isle Rae. They "desired to be held excused at this time, because my Lord Admiral had taken some men and Captain Ando Watson, and other captains had taken others to Denmark and Sweden".

1628. Militia. The barons, gentlemen and Burghs of Fife resolved to raise two regiments of Militia each

---

[31] Gilt.

to be commanded by a gentleman as colonel. The burghs refused to allow their men to serve under a gentleman, or to leave their own bounds unless the shire were invaded by a foreign enemy. This matter was settled by the King's Council intimating that they would themselves appoint officers to command the militia.

Herring Fishing. The Earl of Seaforth proposed to establish a colony of Dutchmen and Flemings at Stornaway, to prosecute the herring fishery; and to have that town erected into a Royal Burgh. These proceedings were looked on with suspicion by the Burghs, and they resolved to oppose them. A kind of joint stock company was formed on the occasion to carry on the herring fishing; but I have no means of ascertaining how far it was carried out.

1629. Plague. The plague prevailing this year in Perth, Orkney and Shetland, the Privy Council interdicted all intercourse with these and other infected places. The Magistrates not having been sufficiently diligent in executing this order, were summoned before the Privy Council to answer for their negligence.

Trade. No exportation of vivers was allowed; therefore Helen Sutherland was fined in five shillings for collecting eggs to be sent to England.

1630. Birth of Charles II. June 6th. There is the following entry – "Understanding that there is an man child born by our Queen to His Majesty on the 29th of May, think it expedient to congratulate the birth of said man child and Prince with praise and thanks to God, and with singing of bells and tooking of drums, and setting forth of bone fires on the streets."

Schoolmaster. Mr Thomas Christie, Schoolmaster, complained to the Council that the School Doctor went from house to house with his scholars, playing at "carts" till 12 o'clock at night. The Council advised them to "patch up the matter, shake hands and drink together" – all which was presently done.

New Quay. The inhabitants were called out to work by turns at the construction of a quay to the east of the Earn Craig.

1633. New Charter. The new charter was this year obtained and sent to Sir John Hay, with three pieces of gold for himself, to be confirmed by Act of Parliament. On the 2nd July the Act was passed, and also another confirming that of James VI, granting 500 merks yearly to the minister.

Banishment. Thomas Phin was banished for ever for being "a drunken beast, and for so misbehaving himself that the lieges cannot live in peace for him".

King crossing the Ferry. July 9 [32]. The King crossed the Firth from Leith on his way to Falkland.[33] On this occasion the Council ordered the officers to have a new suit of clothes, and wine confits and other eatabales to be provided for His majesty and his attendants; the streets to be cleared of middings and red; women and children to keep within doors from morning to night on the day of the King's arrival; two boats with sufficient crews to be got to ferry the King across; and lastly they resolved to admit the King and his attendants free men of the Burgh. On the 10th some of the King's attendants appeared and were with all solemnity admitted, burgesses; but no further notice is taken of the King's journey.

Death of an attendant of the King's. August 3. It is recorded as follows "The Bailies and Council considering that an John Ferries, servant to His Majesty, was found dead within this harbour and brought to land, who died in the boat betwixt this and Leith the time that the King His Majesty was upon the sea betwixt this and Leith, the tent day of July last; and there was found upon the said Jn Ferries the money and others following to wit, of dollars and other white money, forty five pund, twelve shillings; and of gold five twelve pund pieces and one single angel of gold 25 lib 8 shillings and 8 pennies = inde 107 libs, 5 shillings and 4 pennies.

Item; ane ring of gold which was put in the council house.

Item; ane rapier sword with ane belt and hinger.

Item, ane coat and breeks of camblet.

The Bailies think meet that the sums bestowed on his burial be paid to the following persons, viz:-

To Ando Orrock for making graif, 16 shillings.

Item, to John White for ringing the bell, 16 shillings.

Item, to Janet Mair and Elspat Cousin for winding him, 13 shillings.

Item, to William Mitchell for washing his cot and breeks, 16 shillings.

Item, to James Brown, Taylour, 5 elns of linen to be his winding sheet, five pund, 8 shillings.

Item, to David Stirling for making his kist 3 lib, 10 shillings.

Item, to the workmen for carrying him to the tollbooth and after to the kirk, 32 shillings.

Item, to Alexander Barnie for first spying him in the wold, 31 shillings.

August 13. Ane dollar taken out of Mr Ferries' purse to pay for the winding sheet of other man found with

---

[32] This would have been the date of the Town Council's orders. The crossing took place on 10 July.

[33] The King was actually on his way from Falkland, and crossed from Burntisland to Leith.

him."

Sept 17. The Lord Admiral desired the money and other effects which belonged to Mr Ferries to be given up to him.

Dec 24. The affair of the late Mr Ferries, who it appears had been His Majesty's cook, after much negotiating was concluded by the Council obtaining, by what means is not known, the property found on him "to be given to the Kirk Session, deducting alway 40 libs to be given to the Lord Admiral for his gude will in the said money, and the Council think it expedient that the minister and Session build ane seat round the pulpit for sick aged men of the council and Session as cannot well hear the minister's voice".

1635. Dutch Money. The usual mode of counting money at this time was by dollars, rix-dollars and stivers.

Piper. A piper was appointed to go through the town morning and evening.

Death of Lord Melville. August 7. the Council and "honest men" of the Burgh were appointed to "ride" at Lord Melville's funeral at Monimail. They would be greatly grieved no doubt, considering how true a friend they had lost.

Wedderburn's Grammar. The convention ordained that Wedderburn's grammar should be taught in the Burgh Schools. But on the 15th July 1638, this grammar by the same authority was ordered not to be taught in these schools as not being worthy.

About this time there was a writer on grammar of this name belonging to one of the Aberdeen colleges. There was also a very disorderly person residing at Burntisland at this time protected by the Melvilles and Duries, always designated "Master", a title very much limited to Masters of Arts and clergymen. It is possible he may have been the writer referred to.

Port and Street. Measures were taken this year for building the East Port[34], and the inhabitants were called out to assist in causewaying the streets.

Schoolmaster. The Schoolmaster, complained that Mansie Macfeggan and Bessie Davidson keep Schools to the injury of the Grammar School. He shortly after resigned his office, and Mr John Irvine was appointed in his place at the earnest recommendation of the Chancellor, now Archbishop of St. Andrews. The salary was fixed at 100 merks. Fees for teaching Latin; 12 shillings, English; 9 shillings. This Mr Irvine continued through all the changes of government till his death about 1688, and appears to have been held in much esteem.

1636. Book of Common Prayer. Commissioners had been sent to the Convention of Burghs to desire them to supplicate the Lords of the Secret Council to free the Burghs from the obligation of using the Book of Common Prayer, and the Book of Canons. They reported that the nobility had petitioned the Council and had protested against the use of these books and against the Bishops because they could not obtain justice against them. A proclamation was afterwards produced and read from the King, declaring that he was minded to defend the "religion" to the utmost of his power.

Covenant. Feby. 16. It was reported by the Commissioners of the Burgh to the Estates that the nobility, barons, gentlemen, and burgesses had agreed that the Covenant should be subscribed by all ranks, and they desired to know if the Bailies and Council would concur in this. On the 20th of the same month the Council agreed to subscribe the covenant and appointed a deputation to ascertain if the minister, Mr John Mitchelson, would subscribe the covenant and allow it to be read in the kirk; and if he would administer the communion. The minister appeared in the Council and declared <u>nunce rebus stantibus</u> he neither would subscribe the covenant nor allow it to be read in the kirk, nor consent to the continuing of the communion. The Council then consulted the Presbytery, who advised that the neighbours should pass to Kinghorn, where a minister would preach, and where they might subscribe the covenant. The Council "think it not meet to agree to this". The minister, after various proceedings, agreed to allow the covenant to be read in the kirk by the reader, but not on a preaching day. But of this also the Council disapproved.

April 3. The Covenant was ordered to be read at the kirk by "the reader of the Evangel" and subscribed by the inhabitants, burgh and landward. It appears that this order had not been complied with for on the 28th of the same month the Presbytery summoned Mr Mitchelson to answer for disobeying their command, and sent Mr John Smith, minister at Leslie to preach and receive the oaths and subscriptions of the people. The Council requested Orrock of Orrock, Orrock of Bulram, and Ged of Baldrige, to try to persuade the minister to comply with the Presbytery's order. He consented, though as he says, against his will.

Dr Mitchelson. June 26. "Seeing that the people pass to other kirks and will not hear the present minister, and that thereby the poor suffer for want of the usual collections", the Council resolved to have another minister appointed, but they first formally asked Dr Mitchelson if he would distribute the elements in the old manner to the communicants sitting on each side of the table, or if he would allow another minister to dispense the

---

[34] The East Port was completed in 1635.

communion in that way. He refused to allow anything to be done until the Marquis of Hamilton's return, His Majesty having promised that nothing should be done touching the kirk till then. The Council sent to the Earl of Rothes to know if "this be of verity". By his Lordship they were told that "it is not of verity". The minister thereupon was "sharply rebuked", but he maintained the truth of his assertion, and at last allowed James Simpson, minister at Kirkcaldy, to administer the communion in the Presbyterian form.

Mr Wm Livingstone was called to be assistant minister but refused to come.

No Stipend. Dr Mitchelson on asking payment of his stipend, was informed by the Council that there was no money, and that they would not borrow to pay him "unless he would be silent in his doctrine and not rail upon the people as he has done in time past and that he would distribute the elements in the auld manner".

Visitation. Complaints of the "decay of the true religion in the town for want of the preaching of God's Word and the due administration of the Holy Communion", and of the state of want to which the poor were reduced, there being no collections for them at the kirk, having been made to the Presbytery, they resolved to hold a visitation of the kirk, and a "spokesman" was appointed to act for the Council on that occasion. In the meantime the minister informed the Council that he intended to intimate the fast ordered them by the King to be kept before the meeting of the Assembly, and "in respect of the King's proclamation he will dispense the communion to the people sitting round the table", but also declared that whoever teaches that Bishops are unlawful, teaches false doctrine.

1639. The Commissioner sent to the Assembly reported that he had petitioned the Assembly to appoint a helper to Dr Mitchelson "in respect of his infirmities and his stubbornness in not signing the covenant"; and that the assembly had referred the matter to the Presbytery to "tack order with such enormities". Intimation was therefore given to Dr Mitchelson by the Presbytery that he must either subscribe the covenant or be deposed. On the 27th of the same month he was formally accused of the "enormities and erroneous doctrine preached by him for a long time past; of maintaining the articles of Perth, both by word and write, as well in public as by ordinary discourse; of obtaining his son to celebrate the sacraments, he not being lawfully called to the function of the ministry; his not subscribing the covenant and Confession of faith; his speeches against the covenant both in public and private, calling it a black covenant invented by men; saying the Estates at their meeting had pulled the crown off the King's head; maintaining Episcopacy; not catechising; not owning the General Assembly till it be ratified by Parliament; not intimating the sentence against the excommunicated Bishops, notwithstanding his being required to do so by the reverend brethren of the Presbytery.

On the 8th February, Robert Adamson, Reader, reported to the Council "that the Presbytery, by virtue of power given to them by the General Assembly, had deposed Mr John Mitchelson from the office of the ministry; and that they had discharged him from preaching the Word of God; from baptizing or celebrating the elements, and had declared the kirk of this burgh to be vacant; and that the said Mr John is no minister in respect of his disobedience and wilful stubbornness in not subscribing the covenant of God". Mr John thereupon answered that he would teach and use discipline, for all their doings, till he saw the act of deposition. A copy of the act was shown him, and his name does not again appear in the Council record.

This Dr Mitchailson or Mitchelson was a person of learning, and the author of several treatises on ecclesiastical affairs. He seems to have been held in much respect during the earlier part of his incumbency, and had considerable influence in the management of the affairs of the Burgh.

This year Melville of Hall Hill formally abandoned all claim to any part of the land within the Royalty.

East Head. The buildings at the East Head were in progress at this time, the stones being taken from the Ross.

True Religion. The Convention ordered that no person should be admitted a Burgess, elected a Magistrate or sent to Parliament, unless he was of the true "religion".

Arming. During the year 1638 the proceedings of the Council indicated a resolution to resist the government by force. Before this, weapon showings and drillings were held by order of Government; now they were held by order of the Town Council in conjunction with the landward gentlemen of the shire. Drillings were held daily under drill masters sent by the latter. The inhabitants went about their ordinary avocations armed with sword and dagger. Measures were also adapted for fortifying the town.

New Covenant. On the 27th September intimation was received from Edinburgh that a proclamation had been issued by Government, commanding all persons to subscribe the short Confession of Faith, and that solemn proclamations had been made against it. The Council resolved not to subscribe the "New Covenant", and to protest against the "proclamation thereof if it should be made at the cross of the burgh".

Ships. October 24. Two ships from London entered the harbour bound for Aberdeen, suspected to have had "powder and bullet" on board. The Council resolved to detain them if they attempted to sail.

1639. Covenant. February 7. The Presbytery ordered all non-covenanters to subscribe the Covenant "in respect that the General Assembly has declared its will thereanent".

Arming. The nobility and gentry of the shire ordered that the inhabitants be armed and officers appointed;

that "Forths and Strongths" be made, at some of which the parishioners of Aberdour were ordered to assist. The West Broom Hill was accordingly fortified and provided with twenty two men.

Volunteers. May 7. Twenty five men came voluntarily forward and offered to go with the army to the south. The Council ordained that all those who had gone to the "Boundred" should be admitted Burgesses free.

Forced Loan. A forced loan was raised from the inhabitants by the covenanters to bear the expense of the war, the nobility becoming bound for the repayment; but it does not appear that these loans were ever repaid, though often claimed. The sum exacted from each individual was very generally 500 merks. Many made oath that they had no money to lend, and by this means escaped the exaction.

Bribery. Twenty pounds sterling were offered to some person of influence "boun for the court", whose name is left blank in the record, if he should obtain a patent from the King for the admission of Mr Andrew Leslie to be minister of the parish. This measure was successful, but the Presbytery refused to ordain Mr Leslie unless a permanent provision were made for his support.

1640. Intimation was given to the Council that the King had appointed "Northumberland" to command his forces, and to settle the national affairs. No other notice was taken of this communication than to resolve to obtain a supply of ammunition from Holland; and to persevere in holding drillings and weapon showings.

The Council committed their whole powers to the Bailies of this and the past year, because the Council "could not meet in this dangerous time". This was not acted on.

Levies. The Council selected fifteen men to go to the south with Colonel Leslie. Others, but it is not said how many were sent to the north to "Major Colonel Munro". Shortly afterwards the "Council of War of Fife" ordered out every eighth man and another eighth to be in readiness. On the 1st May every fourth man was ordered out, but whether in addition to the former levy does not appear. "A list of valorous men" was sent to the Committee of the shire at Kirkcaldy. The minister gave a list from the communion roll, but stated that many of these were not "able men nor of strength for the war". Every person worth 200 merks was called on to furnish a horse for service. The whole levy is given at forty nine men "besides boys and horses". Along with these all "masterless men, loiterers at home and beggars", were ordered to be sent to the army.

Fortifying and Taxing. The Magistrates were at this time constantly occupied about military affairs. The town was enclosed on all sides. Those leaving it were not allowed to return. Ships attempting to land were ordered to be destroyed. Powder and other munitions of war were searched for and put in a place of safety. The tenth penny of the rent of all heritages within the Burgh was exacted. "Three substantious honest men" were appointed to sit for four hours every day to receive contributions of gold and silver work for the public use.

Runaways. All soldiers who had returned from the army were ordered to be apprehended and sent back, and a new levy was ordered in place of those who had not been found.

Cowards Those men who had been appointed to join the Earl of Dunfermline's regiment and had failed to do so were ordered to be apprehended and stand at the Kirk door with "rock and spindle" in their hands, and a paper on their heads with an inscription in large letters setting forth their "infamy" and to be declared enemies to the true religion, and then banished.

1641. Returned Soldiers. Many persons returned from the army this year. These having been ordered to give up their arms, Lord Balgonie sent a letter to the Council "desiring them not to be so rigourous as to demand Hugh Barclay, trooper, his horse from him, as it was contrary to the law of nations and arms to do so". The Council thought "it no way meet to comply with this request, in respect that there is an Act of Parliament commanding all to give up their arms". It appears, however, that Master Hugh retained his charger, the value of which was said to be 100 merks.

Poverty. The Council ordered that the Minister's stipend should not be collected this year owing to the poverty of the town.

National and local taxes were hitherto collected separately, but it was now resolved to collect them together, and to make up whatever was deficient from the Burgh revenue.

Manse and Glebe. A manse and glebe were ordered by the Presbytery to be provided for the Minister but it does not appear that the order was complied with.

1642. A request being made by the Earl of Irvine that his soldiers should be lodged in the tolbooth, it was refused because the "Council does not know how soon they may need it themselves".

Town and Country. Hitherto little intercourse appears to have been held between the town and landward people, but now the disturbed state of national affairs brought them into closer connection, frequent meetings being held between the Magistrates and county gentlemen for consultation at Kirkcaldy, Dysart, and other places.

Harbour. The Convention of Burghs granted 600 merks for repairs on the harbour.

Plague. The plague prevailing this year in Edinburgh and Leith, the Council complained to the Lords of the Secret Council that the ferry boats from Leith entered the harbour by force, though in some cases they had persons on board who had not passed fifteen days since they were cleansed. A Shipmaster desired to be allowed to land his wife and family they "all being by the blessing of God, in good health". The Council ordered them to remain on board till the full moon. Did they imagine that the moon had influence on the disease?

All persons fit to serve were ordered to be ready to advance for the defence of Dundee against the Athol men.

Fortifying. The Committee of the General Assembly ordered Burntisland and Kirkcaldy to assist at the work.

Convention A meeting of the Convention was appointed to be held at Burntisland in April, because "the sickness still prevails in Edinburgh".

Forts. Sir James Melville desires the Bailies to demolish the forts on the Broom Hill "in respect that he minds to fortify the Castle himself. The Council all in one voice absolutely refuse to do the same."

Quartering. The taxes payable by the town having fallen in arrears, intimation was given that they must be paid under pain of "plundering", a threat which was virtually carried into effect by the quartering of Lord Lindsay's troopers on the town. These soldiers were very disorderly, and very much oppressed the inhabitants.

Tyranny. John Smytton being questioned by the Council, confessed that he had been excommunicated by the Minister of Leith. "The Bailies and Council ordain the said John Smytton, his wife and bairns, household goods and gear whatsoever to be removed furth of this Burgh betwixt this day aught days, under pain of ejection and warding of their persons."

Minister rebuked. "The Council ordain the Minister to be rebukit and to show him that he is very slack and slothful in not giving the communion these four years by past." His name was Smith. He was assistant to the regular minister, who had joined the army in the south whither he also shortly afterwards went.

1645. No Prayers. James Adamson, reader, was "discharged to read the prayers evening and morning hereafter which is done at the direction of the Presbytery of Kirkcaldy conform to the direction book".

Irish rebels. Sir James Wemyss of Bogie, by authority of the Council of War of Fife, ordered all men belonging to the town between 16 and 60 years of age to be ready fully armed to go to Kinross to oppose the Irish rebels who were within six miles of Perth.

1652. Military Rule. There is a blank in the Burgh records from 1646 to 1652. At the latter date the town was in possession of the army of the Commonwealth, and was garrisoned by two and sometimes by three companies of soldiers of about 100 men each, partly horse and partly foot. The town house being occupied by the military, the Burgh Courts were held in a hired house. The community lived under the despotic rule of Colonel Lilburne, the military commander. The Magistrates were subordinate to him, and were employed in little else apparently than raising supplies and providing supplies for his soldiers. No one was allowed to cross the Ferry without a pass from him.

Despotism. Colonel Lilburne intimated to the council by order of the Council of State, that all civil officers were to continue unchanged this year, including the Magistrates and Councillors of the Royal Burgh. This tyrannical proceeding, thus first introduced during the Commonwealth, was followed by Charles II and James VII and was suitable enough to their rule.

1654. Race.[35] During the gloomy time of national and local oppression, the Council instituted a horse race to be run from the East Port to Pettycur on the 29th June (10th July) being St Peter's fair, for a silver cup of 10 ounces weight. No horse was allowed to run above the value of 300 merks. At the same time it was attempted to establish a market for the sale of cattle, but it did not succeed. The race was kept up till about the year 1812.

Church Seats. The landward heritors raised a process to oblige the Council to allocate space in the church on which they might erect seats for their own accommodation. After much controversy the matter was referred to the arbitration of the Laird of Bogie and the Earl of Wemyss, by whom the space under the north and east galleries was assigned to the heritors.

English. There were many English people living in the town at this time, having probably come with Cromwell's soldiers. They refused to pay local taxes and claimed the right of trading, though not burgesses. The Council applied to the General to be allowed to assess these, but the result is not stated.

Streets and Harbour. Causewaying the streets and repairing the harbour works were now renewed. "The strong men and women" were called out to labour at these works by turns. To bear the expense 584 pounds were raised by assessment on the inhabitants. Some contributions were made by the neighbouring Burghs, and six months' government assessment was directed to be applied to the same purpose.

Perhaps this last contribution has given rise to the report that the streets were causewayed and the harbour works repaired by Cromwell. But the whole of his contribution for these purposes amounted to only 33 pounds sterling.

---

[35] It is now generally accepted that the first horse race took place in 1652.

Poverty. So severely were the annoyances arising from the town being occupied by the soldiers of the Commonwealth felt, that almost all the craftsmen left it. Most of the work done for the inhabitants was done by workmen from Aberdeen. The revenue of the burgh was not sufficient to pay the interest of its debt, and an assessment was levied on the inhabitants to enable the council to meet that charge. Repeated applications were made to the General for relief, but without effect.

Bringing home the King. From this time to the year 1656 many notices appear in the Burgh records about raising funds for paying the expense "of bringing home the King from Holland". These proceedings can only refer, as I can conceive, to the coming of Charles II to Scotland in 1650. But how they came to be countenanced by the government of the time is not easy to imagine. The following is the substance of these notices:-

1562. [36] Sixteen pounds ordered to be paid to John Brown for "wine and other furniture" expended in his house to the town's use when the King was travelling with his servants.

1656. Sep 26. David Seaton made report that at the Convention of Burghs of Fife, which met at Dysart, Lord Brodie and Alexander Jaffray, Provost of Aberdeen, produced a warrant from the Lord Protector for levying a month's assessment from each Burgh for the expense of bringing home the King from Holland, and which assessment they desired to be ready by the last day of the month.

On the 22nd of the same month another meeting was held on the same subject by appointment of Mr Thomas Glover, "anent the month's maintenance ordered by the late Parliament to be paid to the commissioners who brought home the King". On this occasion the matter was referred to a meeting to be held at Cupar on the 15th of October.

November 17. A report was given in of a meeting of the Burghs with Provost Jaffray of Aberdeen, anent the month's maintenance demanded by him and his partners for bringing home the King. A meeting was appointed to be held at Dysart on the same subject.

Nov 24. It is reported that the Fife Burghs met at Dysart and that the meeting was unfrequented, but that those met had resolved to pay a month's assessment to Provost Jaffray for bringing home the King. The Council agreed to this for this Burgh and ordered the same to be collected from the inhabitants. The month's assessment for Burntisland amounted to about sixteen pounds sterling.

Westminster Parliament. August 4. Each of the Burghs of Fife ordered to send a Commissioner to Cupar to elect a Commissioner to represent the Burghs in Parliament to be held at Westminster. The Commissioners met accordingly, but, before proceeding with the elections they resolved to consult their several Burghs regarding the penalty imposed on unqualified persons voting thereat. The qualification referred to was that they had not aided or abetted in any way against the State since the year 1640. The penalty was forfeiture of one year's income and half their personal property. Andro Smith was appointed Commissioner to vote for Burntisland, and he accepted the charge on condition that the Council would relieve him of any injury that he might suffer in consequence.

On the 17th James Sword was elected to represent the Fife Burghs, and was to be allowed seventy two pounds sterling to bear his charges; but if other members had less than twenty shillings a day, he was to refund whatever of his allowance exceeded this. Mr Sword was very much dissatisfied with his allowance, and quarrelled with his constituents about it. The Convention, interfered to compose the difference between the parties. I have not seen any other notice of this Mr Sword, but he appears to have been a person of a mean disposition.

Brewers. Brewers were forbidden to make malt or brew on Sabbath without licence of the Bailies. These were a numerous body. On one occasion sixty one were fined for selling "dear ail", that was for selling ale above the 12 pennies (about ¼d sterling for an English pint). The dear ale was of a better quality than could be sold at the statutory price.

Soldiers. Forty six pounds sterling were distributed monthly by the Council among such of the inhabitants as had soldiers quartered on them. They were authorised to assess the inhabitants for this, but as no more than £20 sterling could be raised in this way monthly, the rest was taken from the Burgh funds or borrowed on the security of the Burgh property. By this means the town was brought to the verge of bankruptcy. This money was advanced under the name of "coal and candle money". It was a debt against the government, and though often claimed was never fully repaid. In order to relieve the town, the brewers agreed to submit to an assessment of ten shillings on the boll of malt, but it could not be collected. Charles II on his accession granted power to levy a similar assessment, but this was found to exceed his authority.

2 Pennies on the Pint. An Act of Parliament was obtained after the Revolution for levying 2 pennies on the pint on ale used in the Burgh. This Act was for a limited time, but was periodically renewed till a recent

---

[36] The date is incorrect, and was changed in pencil to 1655.

period.

Shore Dues. Sept 12. A regular table of shore dues and small customs was published for the first time.

Slander. Janet Haldane was ordained to stand at the cross with "a vile slanderer" inscribed on a paper on her head, for slandering Isobel Burnet.

1654. Jurisdiction. The Burgesses at this time claimed to be exempt from the jurisdiction of the Sheriff and Commissary.

Frivolous Lawsuits. In order to prevent frivolous lawsuits the Bailies were authorized to decide all causes under ten shillings sterling by a verbal hearing of the parties. Money seemed at this time to be occasionally reckoned by sterling.

1655. Emigration. So severely oppressed by the presence of the military and the assessments for their support that many emigrated, chiefly to Aberdour. Amongst these the Town Clerk had gone there and refused to return unless security were given that he would be exempted from "quartering and watching and warding". To this the council agreed, and each councillor signed a minute in the council record. Judging from the handwriting of the members, they were all respectably educated, better, by the same rule, than their successors one hundred and fifty years later.

Profanity. The laws against "profane swearing, cursing, scolding, mocking of piety, filthy speaking, drinking to excess and compelling others to drink", were ordered by the Magistrates to be put in execution, "and that without prejudice to the censures of the Kirk".

Manse. It having been represented that the Minister's manse was worth only 30 pounds, and that he ought to have one worth 60 pounds, the Council agreed to pay 20 libs, and the heritors to "mortify" 250 merks, the annual rent of which was to be for the remainder.

Kidnapping. June 18. Colonel Fairfax (the military commandant, I imagine) required the Council to apprehend and give up to him all idle men and women between the ages of twenty and forty years, in order to be sent to Barbadoes. Clothes were to be supplied to those in want of them and a groat a day allowed to each till they were received on shipboard. The Council refused to comply till they knew if the gospel were preached at Barbadoes.

No Bailies. None of the persons elected to be Bailies this year would accept of the office, apparently from the embarrassed state of the town's affairs, arising from the great number of soldiers to be provided for and from the control exercised by the military commanders over the Magistrates. The Council in these circumstances elected a Moderator to preside in the council in place of the Magistrates, and supplicated the council of State to interfere.

Four Bailies. Next year four Bailies appeared in office, but how or by whom appointed does not appear.

1656. Member of Parliament. August 20. Colonel Nathanius Wathane, an Englishman, was elected by deputies from the Fife Burghs to represent them in a Parliament to be held at Westminster. On this occasion there is no reference to wages, but these Burghs presented £100 sterling to him.

Despotism. the headquarters of the military force was at this time at the Castle of Burntisland. Captain Roger, the officer in command, sent an imperative order to the Magistrates to send four beds for him and his attendants.

Richard proclaimed Protector. An order was sent from the Sheriff to proclaim the Lord Protector. The order was complied with, but with what formalities is not recorded. The minute in the record is obscurely written, perhaps intentionally. The inhabitants could not favour the Commonwealth, considering the oppressions they had suffered from it.

Woman Teacher. Mary Malpas was allowed a free house and school house for teaching "young lassies".

1658. The School Doctor was dismissed because he could not teach arithmetic nor the rudiments of grammar, and from being Session Clerk because he was "unfit".

Kirkcaldy and Culross. A commissioner was sent to Kirkcaldy to meet with Commissioners from other towns, to settle the constitution of that Burgh and to establish a Guildry there; and another Commissioner sent to Culross for a similar purpose.

1659. Strangers. The acts against harbouring strangers were renewed. The inhabitants were ordered not to let their houses to any but "honest famous persons". The adherents of the Stewarts appeared to be moving, and achange of government being suspected, caused this increased vigilance.

General Monk. A supplication was sent to General Monk, praying for recompense for the greater number of soldiers quartered on the town than its due proportion. It was rejected, but in his answer he said the soldiers would be all removed in a short time.

Monk's Deception. Nov 7. A letter was received from "The Lord General" requesting a Commissioner to be sent to meet him at Edinburgh to consult about matters concerning the country. A Commissioner was sent accordingly, and reported on his return that the Lord General had advised the Magistrates to preserve "the Peace of the Commonwealth" within the Burgh; authorized them to suppress all tumults, and unlawful assemblings;

and desired them to hold no communication with any of Charles Stewart's party, but to apprehend any such as made disturbances, and to send them to the next garrison. Further, he desired them to encourage and countenance a godly ministry, and all that truly fear God in the land; and finally he advised them to continue faithfully to own and assert the interest of the parliamentary government, and to send him word to Berwick by the 12th of December how far they will comply with his desires.

An answer to this communication, signed by such of the Councillors as approved of it, was sent to the Lord General and delivered to Sir James Stewart. The words of the answer are not recorded, but it seemed to be favourable to the wishes of the General, or rather what he desired to be believed that he wished for the occasion, for on the 26th of December a letter was received from the Town Clerk of Edinburgh, with a copy of one addressed by Monk to the Council of Edinburgh and those of certain other Burghs, giving them hearty thanks for their respect to the Commonwealth and himself, and for the good interest now contended for, promising to keep a grateful sense of the same, and to give protection to them and all other Burghs.

Restoration of Charles II. May 16. Intimation was received from the Provost of Edinburgh that the Parliament had resolved to bring back the King, and requesting a commissioner to be sent to consult about that matter. A letter was received at the same time from the "correspondent" of the Burghs in London, appointing the 29th May for the meeting, and desiring the Commissioner to bring along with him the town's part of £1000 sterling for promoting the interest of the Burghs at this juncture; all which orders were complied with and the following proclamation issued by the Council.

Proclamation. "Forasmikle as several persons disaffected to the King's Majesty do wickedly speak opprobrious words of His Highness, thereby showing their disloyalty and unwillingness to submit and subject themselves to his Majesty's just and lawful authority rightfully belonging to His Highness over all people of this nation, for the suppressing of which insolence in time to come and for the admonition of the people living in this place that they fall not into such snares; the Bailies and Council ordain and command all persons within this Burgh of whatsoever kind or degree that they nor none of them presume to speak any such words approbrious [sic] or dishonourable to His Majesty in any manner of way under the pain of being summarily apprehended and accused of treason."

£1000 Sterling to the King. May 28. A letter was received from the Agent of the Burghs at London, intimating that the King had accepted of the £1000 before alluded to, and desiring that it might be paid "his bills". The Burgh's proportion of this sum was 200 pounds Scots. The treasurer on being ordered to collect it by assessment, refused, on which he was fined 50 pounds and incarcerated; but was afterwards released on his expressing his readiness to make the collection.

English Officers. A Councillor was expelled from the Council for saying that the Bailies had wasted the common good by paying 55 pounds of lawen at the admitting of the English officers to be Burgesses. The Bailies asserted that this was to gain the favour of the English, and thereby promote the public interest. The offender was restored on asking pardon.

Watch and Ward. The inhabitants were called out by the Magistrates for the first time for several years to watch and ward. The town had during the Commonwealth been under a military despotism.

Homicide. Alexander Boswell, Skipper in Kirkcaldy, was killed by Peter Bettwood, a trooper of Captain Fermer's company. After examining witnesses, the Bailies at the desire of the Captain surrendered the accused to him; but how he was afterwards disposed of is not recorded.

A complaint was made to Major General Morgan that the troopers went through the town nightly, and stopped persons going about their lawful affairs. The General answered that they would soon have as great freedom as heretofore, referring apparently to the withdrawing of the soldiers on the restoration of the King.

Conventicles. Aug 16. Proclamation was made by order of the committee of Estates, forbidding all unlawful meetings or conventicles, and all seditious petitions.

Englishmen. Another, forbidding all insolences to be committed on Englishmen, was also issued.

"Lex Rex" etc. Sept 14. Proclamation for suppressing the seditious pamphlets called "Lex Rex" and "The causes of God's wrath"; against meetings without warrant, and against pasquils against his Majesty, were issued.

Minister confined. Sept 16. The Minister of the parish had been confined in the Castle of Edinburgh. A commission was sent by the Town Council to supplicate the Committee of Estates for his liberation. This had been ineffectual, for the application was renewed on the 24th of the month; on this occasion setting forth that he was in infirm health, and praying that if he could not be liberated, he might be confined at Burntisland. This also was disregarded for a new application was made on the 29th October, but with what effect is not said.

Remonstrance. A letter was received from the Chancellor ordering that no person who had signed the "remonstrance", or who was known to be disaffected towards the King be elected Magistrate, Councillor or deacon.

"Doytes". Those who refused to receive the "Doytes" for one penny, as ordered by the King's proclamation, were to be fined in forty shillings.

1661. Oath of Allegiance. The oath of allegiance was taken by the Councillors. I have not observed that such an oath had been administered before.

Coronation. All persons were ordered to set out bonfires on the streets before their doors in honour of the King's coronation in England.

Declaration. "The Declaration" acknowledging the King's supremacy in all matters and over all persons, civil and ecclesiastical, was at this time offered for subscription to all persons in office, including the Magistrates, Councillors and other men in office in the Burghs. "The Declaration" was contrary to that principle which rejects the authority of the civil power in matters ecclesiastical; and rather than acknowledge the existence of such, many of all ranks now suffered persecution. By the abuse of his power, the King had brought the established church to the external form of Episcopacy but there was no sincere acquiescence, scarcely indeed the appearance of it, amongst the inhabitants of Burntisland. The reluctance of the Town Councillors to subscribe the "Declaration" appears from their deferring from time to time to do so, for what seems very inadequate reasons. Their fear of giving offence to the government appears also from the fact that they never directly or formally refused. The following extracts from the record refer to this matter:-

1662. Oct 6. The Declaration sent by the Sheriff Depute of Fife to be subscribed by the Bailies and Councillors. "The Council in respect of the infrequency of the meeting, defer the consideration of this matter."

Oct 19. "The Declaration read in the face of the Council by the Clerk, but none would subscribe it, whereupon he took instruments", that is, he protested that he had done what he had been required to do, and relieved himself from being blamed in the matter.

Dec 7. The Declaration sent by the Privy Council to be subscribed by the Town Council. "The Council in respect that they are not frequently met, ordain the whole Council to meet this day eight days." The eight days passed, but no subscription was made. A letter was received from the Chancellor and one from the Clerk of the Privy Council, both referring to the same matter, and both urging the subscription. The affair was long deferred from one meeting to another, for which various reasons were assigned, very like pretences. At last the document was subscribed, but not in testimony of their belief of the truth of the principles set forth in it, but, as they express it, "in testimony of their loyalty". Even this qualified acquiescence was sufficient to deter many from accepting the office of Magistrate or Councillor; and for a long time after this a sufficient number could not be found to make up the legal number of Councillors. They, however, acted as if the Council were full.

1663. Church vacant. The Church was at this time vacant, and the Council applied to "my Lord the Bishop of St Andrews" to send a minister to supply the vacancy.

1664. Harbour Works. The works at the harbour were still incomplete, and a warrant was obtained from the Privy Council for a voluntary contribution through the Burghs to assist in repairing and extending them. The following was the result:-

Edinburgh gave 280 libs, Aberdeen 186 libs, Leith 41 libs, Arbroath 20 libs, Cannongate 33 libs, 6 shillings, Anstruther 29 libs, Glasgow 120 libs, Kilrenny 13 libs, 16 shillings, Anstruther Wester, 6 libs, Pittenweem 20 libs, Crail 29 libs; in whole 818 libs, 2 shillings. I have not seen it recorded how this money was laid out.

Peterhead. 53 libs were collected at the kirk door to be sent to Peterhead towards the expense of repairing the harbour of that place.

Bishops. The Bishops of Edinburgh and Dunkeld were admitted Burgesses. These prelates are styled in the margin of the record "My Lords Edinburgh and Dunkeld".

Royal Navy. The fabric of the Church was at this time upheld by the kirk session, and the expense taken from the "penalties box".

Sept 5. Twelve men were sent to the Royal Navy, being the town's proportion of 500 ordered to be levied in Scotland. None could be found to go voluntarily, and the Council selected whom they pleased. A few days afterwards ten more were required, but the council deferred the consideration of the matter "till a more frequent meeting". The men, however, were ultimately procured.

Anchorage. The Council by their own authority established a table of anchorage. A ferry yawl was to pay 2 pennies; a boat with deck 6/8; ships under 10 tons 10/8; larger vessels according to their tonnage to those of 200 tons and upwards which were to pay £3"6"8. Foreign ships were to pay one third more than Scotch.

1665. Plague. the plague prevailing in London, Holland and other foreign places, no foreign ships were allowed to have intercourse with the town.

Imprisonment. Three women were imprisoned till they told who were the fathers of their illegitimate children.

1666. Murder. A murder was committed by William Moncrieff, Tailor, on William Brown of Dunbar, by stabbing him with a whanger. The Bailies found that they had not authority to try the accused, and therefore applied to his Grace the Commissioner, and the Lord Justice General for advice. The Council desired that if the said William be convicted, he should suffer here. By a Privy Council warrant he was taken to Edinburgh, and there is nothing further recorded regarding him.

Military levy. There was a general arming going on at this time. Each person was ordered to declare what arms he possessed, and to repair to the Kirk Wynd with them. Arms were ordered to be provided for those who had none. There were 205 men enrolled as volunteers, of whom 42 were equipped at the town's expense. Of these two thirds were musketeers and bandiliers, and one third armed with picks only.

Militia. "All good fellows" who would volunteer (for permanent service, I presume) were ordered to be made freemen and relieved from assessments while in the service; to have their arms and four rix dollars in hand. It is stated that each musket cost 8 merks; each "Bell of bandiliers", 24 shillings; & each pike, 2 shillings. The whole cost to the Burgh was 185 libs. There was an assessment levied on the inhabitants to bear the expense of providing colours, drums, halberds, and livery coats. The whole levy were ordered to rendezvous at Auchtertool. They were called "Militia".

1667. Dutch Attack. May. The town was attacked by a Dutch Squadron, but it does not appear that much damage was done. The Council appealed to the Lord Commissioner for arms to repel any fresh attack. Some great guns, with suitable ammunition, were sent. All fencible men were ordered to be armed; and some who had fled from the town during the attack were ordered to be punished.

Sabbath. At this time repeated orders were issued by the Council for enforcing the strict observance of the Sabbath. No boats were allowed to cross the ferry, nor any horses to be hired for inland journeys without leave from the Bailies. These regulations continued in force till towards the end of last century.

Polonian Minister. "Mr John Elsher, Polonian Minister", represented to the council "that he had been obliged to leave his country, parents, friends and church, all at the hands of the bloody papists"; and craved leave to solicit contributions for his support, which request was granted.

1669. Town's Agent. Sir George Mackenzie was appointed Town's Agent at a salary of 20 merks yearly.

Beggars. Owing to the incr ease of the number of beggars and robbers, watching and warding were strictly enforced on the inhabitants.

Harbour. Application was made to The Convention for a grant of money to be expended on the works connected with the harbour, the maintaining of which being, as the Council sets forth, "a burden almost intolerable".

1670. "Miln". Peter Walker of Dunfermline offered to erect a "miln" to be driven by horses, but was not allowed.

May 29. The King's birthday and Restoration day were ordered to be kept by setting out fires on the streets.

Minister. Oct 2. A Commissioner sent to "My Lord St. Andrews" to request him to provide "a good Minister for the parish in place of Mr William Livingston deceased", reported on his return that "the Bishop had promised to take special care to have an able Minister provided". My Lord, however, seems to have forgotten his promise or an able minister was not to be had, for the application was renewed with the concurrence of the landward gentlemen. The church had for several years been vacant, and the stipend granted to the University of St Andrews. The first notice in the Council record after this regarding a minister is in the year 1677 when Mr George Clerk appears as minister, but when or by whom appointed is not said.

1671. Levy of Soldiers. A levy of 82 men from the shire was ordered by Government to serve in the army, of whom the Burghs were to raise 20, and of these, 3 men were to be provided by Burntisland and Kirkcaldy jointly.

Levies of Seamen. 500 seamen were ordered to be raised in Scotland, of whom 12 were appointed to be raised by Burntisland. The Council offered three rix dollars of bounty to each man who would enter voluntarily; but if the number could not be obtained in that way the Bailies were authorized to secure them in any way they thought fit. Shipmasters were fined if they allowed their servants to escape. To bear the expense of these levies each fencible man was obliged to pay thirty shillings.

1672. Regality of Dunfermline. The Earl of Dunfermline as Bailie of the Regality of Dunfermline continued to assert his superiority over the town and to summon the Burgesses to do service at the head court of the Regality. Against these proceedings the Council obtained an Act of Suspension from the Privy Council, and a process of declarator was afterwards instituted to have it found that the town was independent of the Regality. This was obtained and all claims of superiority was abandoned by the Earl about 1680.

Debtors. An Act was passed at this time for abolishing the right of Burgesses to arrest their debtors within Burgh, unless it were for "meat, drink or horse-meat".

Free Trade. An Act was passed to allow the Burgesses of Burghs of Regality and Barony to Export goods the produce of this country, and to import foreign commodities to the value thereof, very much to the displeasure of the Royal Burgesses. This act was repealed a short time after the Revolution. Why it was enacted, and being enacted – for it was a step, though a short one, in the direction of free trade – why it was repealed, I do not see stated.

1673. Declaration. April. The Lord Chamberlain (Lauderdale) intimated to the Magistrates that the Lords of the Secret Council had "laid on him" to ascertain who of the Magistrates and Councillors of the Fife Burghs had taken and who had not taken, the Declaration at the last election and to report the result to them. He also requested the Council, if they had not subscribed the Declaration, to meet together and do so, and then to transmit it to the Laird of Balbie this day, or to himself at Edinburgh tomorrow before 12 o'clock. He also desired that the names of such as were absent or refused to give obedience to this order be transmitted to him. The council met accordingly and a copy of the Declaration was offered for subscription to all who had not formerly subscribed it. On investigation it was found that all the Bailies and five of the Councillors had signed it in 1664. There were four present who had not subscribed and eight were absent. Whether or not the other parts of Lauderdale's orders were complied with is not stated. At the following election of Councillors it is recorded that the Declaration was produced. Some of the Council appear to have subscribed it, some refused on the ground that they had done so before, and some said that they would consider the matter. In the year 1676 four persons were fined in 100 pounds each for refusing to accept of office in the Council on account of this obnoxious document, and declared incapable of holding any office thereafter. In 1677 a charge of horning was served on the council collectively at the instance of His Majesty's Advocate, because the members had refused to "take the Declaration". In consequence of these proceedings the number of Councillors seldom exceeded ten, being all that could be obtained.

Conventicles. The Magistrates had received strict orders to prosecute all frequenters of Conventicles. In place, however, of exacting the prescribed fines in money from those convicted of such offences, they took bonds for the amount with the intention as was suspected, of not exacting payment. For this offence the Bailies were called to answer before the Commissioner of the Privy Council at Cupar, and informed there that if they neglected to prosecute conventiclers, or took bonds in place of money from convicted recusants, they would be concussed by the Privy Council. Not withstanding these threatenings, it appears that the law or orders of the Privy Council in these matters were not fully carried into effect this time.

Intercommuning. In 1678 an Act of the Chancellor was presented to the Council enjoining all noblemen, gentlemen, Magistrates and Town Councillors to subscribe a bond engaging not to hold conventicles or private meetings. The Council deferred the consideration of this till next meeting. It was then subscribed by one Bailie and seven Councillors, being all that were present. A short time after this a new bond was presented, the same as the former, but with the addition that the subscribers were not to commune with forfaulted person, or with ministers of vacant parishes (whose ministers had been ejected, I imagine). This bond was subscribed by the Clerk, Schoolmaster and eleven Councillors. One present refused, and three were absent. The Burgesses who had refused to accept of the office of Councillor were fined in 100 pounds each; but there were other recusants.

Recusants. The whole of the Town Council were ordered to attend the Magistrates to the Church, preceded by the officers with halberds. This appears to have been devised as a means of compelling them to countenance the new order of ecclesiastical government. The custom of the Magistrates going in procession to the church was introduced in this manner and was continued till very lately, though with less pomp and circumstance than in early times. The Council, which now numbered only eleven, appears to have been quite purified of covenanters and conventiclers, and zealously carried out the decrees of the Government. They ordered all private schools to be shut up. "All disorderly persons who will not give obedience to the Act of Parliament but withdraw themselves from public ordinances" were ordered to "remove themselves, their wives and bairns from the town within 24 hours under pain of ejection and other pains that may follow".

Prayers. Up to the time of the Restoration there were prayers at the opening of each meeting of the Council, but after that time there is no reference to that custom, nor am I aware that it was ever resumed. I shall now return to 1674.

1674. Ransom for Captives. A letter was received from Inverkeithing with a copy of an act of the Privy Council, authorizing a contribution for the ransom of three sailors detained by the Turks in Salec, of whom one belonged to Burntisland. The ransom was said to be 500 or 600 dollars for each. The Council authorised the contribution, and desired the minister to intimate it from the pulpit.

Non-resident Commissioners. A letter was addressed by the King to the Burghs forbidding them to send non-residenters to Parliament or the Convention. They did not say that they would comply and in their answer they complained of the regulations for exacting custom and of the admission of Burghs of Regality and Barony to the privileges of Royal Burghs.

1677. Ferries. The Burgh of Kinghorn desired Burntisland to join with it in a petition to the Privy Council to have the towns of Dysart and Kirkcaldy prevented from plying the ferry to Leith. This desire was complied with and the matter was referred by the Privy Council to the Court of Session to have the question of right determined. The Court appointed three of their number to confer with the parties to get them to agree. In this they were unsuccessful, but persuaded them to refer the matter to Sir William Bruce and Sir John Ramsay as arbiters. These disagreeing, gave no deliverance. Some time after, James Crawford of Mountquhanny and Robert Beatson of Kilrie were appointed, with Sir John Cunningham of Carpington as Oversman. These arbiters also disagreed, and Sir John decided that Kirkcaldy was to be allowed four ferry boats and no more, but that notwithstanding his decree it would be lawful for the two Burghs to apply to Parliament to have Kirkcaldy altogether excluded. This decreet appears to have been acquiesced in, but there does not seem to have been any application to Parliament on the subject. The proceedings were very long and complicated. The final deliverance was not given till 1683. Dysart is not referred to in the Council record.

1679. Duke of Monmouth. Half a barrel of powder was ordered to be bought "wherewith to compliment the Duke of Monmouth on his return from the Wemyss".

Drummer and Violers. The town drummer beat his drum daily through the town at 7 o'clock in the morning and 4 o'clock in the afternoon. There was also a town "violer". The latter complained that the violers living without the Burgh came in and played on "bass and triple viols to his prejudice". These external violers were forbidden to play within the Burgh.

Trades. Previous to this time admission as a Burgess entitled the individual to all corporate privileges, but now the craftsmen divided themselves into associations according to their occupations; and ostensibly for the purpose of providing for their own poor, they desired to be allowed to compel all workmen within the Burgh to contribute to their funds or to cease from working. The Council refused to grant this. In 1681 the Bakers and Wrights petitioned the Privy Council to compel the Town Council to grant the privileges referred to, as they caled them, and to allow them to elect deacons with a right to a place in the Council. The prayer of this petition being refused, all the crafts, namely, the Masons, Wrights, Tailors, Websters, Baxters, Showemakers and Fleshers, petitioned the Court of Session to the same effect. This Court found that the Council was not obliged to grant them charters, but ordained that a visitor should be appointed by each trade to prosecute unfree or unqualified workmen before the Burgh Court, and to exact six pennies from "extraneous" workmen for every pound they earned. In 1683 the seven trades were regularly incorporated, voluntarily, I presume, by the Town Council, with the usual exclusive privileges and officers; but their deacons had not a place in the Council in right of their offices. It was agreed that in future the Council should consist of fourteen ordinary Burgesses, and one of each of the seven trades but all elected by the Council. The craftsmen were thus constituted a distinct order in the Burgh. They were proud of their "order", and stood as firmly by it as any Peer did by his, looking on all unfree men as quite an inferior class. In 1832 all their privileges and distinctions, which, however, had for long been wavering, for ever disappeared. In 1728 the Guildry was established giving its members the exclusive right of trading within the Burgh. The management of its affairs was committed to the Dean of Guild and six Councillors elected by the Town Council. The Dean was a Magistrate, having, with his Council, jurisdiction in mercantile causes, in questions about boundaries and about weights and measures.

Tax on Coals. Twelve pennies were exacted by order of the Council for each load of coals brought into the town, to be applied towards the expense of causewaying the streets. This tax continued for many years.

1682. Freight. The ferriers were authorized to take four shillings from each passenger, if above the degree of a servant; and two shillings for each if of that degree.

Collection for the Harbour. A general collection was authorised this year by the Privy Council, for repairing the harbour of Burntisland "which is of such general and great importance"; and the archbishops and Bishops were desired to require each minister to intimate it from his pulpit.

Thirlage. A long and complicated negotiation was entered into with the Countess of Wemyss regarding the thirlage of the Sea Mills to the right of which she had succeeded, the Burgh disputing her right to levy it, but it led to no settlement.

Windmill. There was a pro posal to erect a Windmill on the Lammerlaws for the purpose of evading the thirlage, but it was not carried into effect.

Teind of Fish. June 16. The Archbishop of St Andrews gave a commission to the minister of the parish. Mr George Clerk, to exact the teind of fish brought into the town. The Council wrote to "His Grace" to know "by what authority". In the following September a protest was entered into against this exaction as being without the "shadow of right". "His Grace" confessed that he had no legal right and would not trouble the town any more about it. The payment of the 500 merks by the Exchequer was finally withdrawn at this time; and the attempt to take the teind of fish was probably meant to supply the want of this allowance.

Military Levy. All men between 16 and 60 years old, fit for military service, were ordered to be in readiness for his Majesty's service; and each householder was ordained to pay four shillings to provide for their equipment. Formerly those who served in the militia were exempt from local taxes, but now, owing, as it is stated, to the poverty of the town, they were obliged to pay these.

King's Birthday. King James VII ordered his own birthday to be celebrated by the setting out of bonfires and the ringing of bells.

Claim of Inverkeithing to Custom. The town of Inverkeithing made a claim for custom from this and all other Burghs on the north side of the Forth between the water of Decon and the town of Leven. Inverkeithing carried the cause to the Court of Session, and a proof was allowed. The Magistrates went to Inverkeithing to commune with the authorities there, and on their return reported that the action was to be abandoned. Notwithstanding this, decree was given against Burntisland. On this the town's charter was exhibited in court, and the decree was recalled. This cause was revived in 1688 but ultimately abandoned, on what ground I have not seen recorded.

1686. Free Trade The King ordered the Convention to ascertain the number of ships belonging to Scotland, with the intention of establishing a free trade with England; but how that was expected to promote such a measure is not said. The Convention, in their answer, set forth that the privileges, of trading to foreign parts had been conferred on Burghs of Regality and Barony without subjecting them to the taxes borne by the Royal Burghs; that every cause between one Royal Burgh and another must now be taken before the Privy Council in place of being referred, as formerly, to the friendly arbitration of neighbouring towns. These grievances they submitted to his Majesty for redress, but assured him of their resolved loyalty whatever might be his decision thereanent. The Viscount Melfort wrote in answer that the King would commit the redress of these grievances to Parliament, and said that he trusted they in turn would support the "best of Kings and benefactors".

No Election. The Chancellor intimated to the Council that by order of the King the Magistrates now in office were to continue till his Majesty's pleasure should be signified. This measure was taken lest persons disaffected to government should get into power.

Aristocratic Insolence. Sept 27. the Earl of Tweeddale, Bailie of the Regality of Dunfermline, claimed 550 pounds as arrears of feu duty, and at the same time cited one of the Bailies for refusing to provide a boat to carry Mr Hay, Writer to the Signet, to Leith. The first action appears to have been a punishment for the crime of not attending to the wants of Mr Hay, no doubt one of his Lordship's clan. The first was advocated to the Court of Session; the other was met by a Bill of Suspension from the Privy Council.

1687. Tyranny. June. The Earl of Balcarras appeared personally at the Council with a letter from the King authorising him to appoint Magistrates, and these to appoint Councillors, to serve till Michaelmas; but at Michaelmas they were all ordered to continue during his Majesty's pleasure.

Kirkcaldy and Dysart. The Burghs of Kirkcaldy and Dysart applied to the convention to be relieved of government taxes – the former on account of the decay of trade; the latter because my Lord Sinclair had taken their crafts and harbour from them by process of law.

Dutch Fishing. Complaints were made to Government that great injury was suffered by the Dutch being allowed to fish within sight of land, contrary to existing treaties.

Expiring Tyranny. The inhabitants were in great distress at this time owing to the losses sustained by the capture of many of their ships during the war with Holland, and the expense they were subjected to for the maintenance of soldiers and prisoners quartered on the town, and in transporting them to Leith. A representation on the subject having been made the Earl of Balcarras, in place of giving relief, intimated that unless the government assessments were paid, he would quarter more troops on the town – no vain threat as the inhabitants knew by experience. Therefore, to prevent the entire ruin of the town, the Council, after various expedients had been tried, borrowed money from the Kirk Session, Prime Guild[37] and private persons, till their credit was exhausted, to enable them to pay the tax or so much of it as could not be collected from the inhabitants.

1688. Minister. The Parish Minister having died, application was made to the Archbishop to provide a good and pious minister for the Parish.

Militia. The County Militia were called out, and ordered to rendezvous at Kirkcaldy. Of this levy, Burntisland sent ten men, and an assessment of five shillings was exacted from each family to bear the expense of equipping them and furnishing them with forty days provisions.

Birth of the Pretender. July 28. By order of the King, bon-fires were set out and the bells rung "to congratulate the birth of an high and mighty prince, the Prince and Stewart of Scotland".

Fencible Men. Dec 31. The whole fencible men were ordered to meet in the Links in their best array.

1689. Prince of Orange. The declaration of the Prince of Orange was read at the cross with great solemnity. Bon-fires were ordered to be set out, and the tollbooth bell to be rung. There is no mention of the ringing of the Kirk bell on this occasion. There is here left a blank page in the Council record and the minute referring to this event is not signed by the Bailies, as was required to render it valid.

Military Array. Jany. 21. The inhabitants were at this time divided into two companies for military service. 84 pounds having been paid to Bailie Seaton for supplying the Ministers with "meat and drink" who

---

[37] Gilt.

came to officiate during the vacancy in the church, he, in place of appropriating this money to his own use, bought a stand of colours with it having the town's armorial bearings painted on them, and presented them to the inhabitants.

Feby. 4. The Magistrates and Councillors in office, who had been all appointed by the late Government, proceeded to elect a new council, by what authority is not said. This election was cancelled, and a new election by authority of the Privy council appointed to be made on the 8th of April, by all those "bearing burden", excluding pensioners, servants and bedsmen.

This election was also annulled because some non-residents had voted at it, amongst whom Robertson of Newbigging is specified, and some who had not taken the oath of allegiance to King William and Queen Mary. On the 29th September an election by poll vote was effected and the municipality was restored to its old condition.

Universal Suffrage. March 4. A letter was presented from King William addressed to the Clerk, ordering him to call a meeting of the inhabitants to elect a Commissioner to Parliament. The inhabitants met accordingly, and elected "unanimously all but ten persons" Bailie Ged. Bailie Ged had been one of King James' Magistrates.

Accounts. At this time, as if there had been a fear of investigation, there were clearings up of accounts and giving discharges to those who had been concerned in the administration of Burghal affairs during the late reign.

King's Birth-day. Novr 4. the birth-day of King William, and the anniversary of his arrival in England were ordered to be kept in the same way as that of Charles II.

Act against Profanity. The council enacted as follows:- "Albeit that by several Acts of Parliament, cursing, swearing, excessive drinking, profaning the Sabbath, mocking the worship of God and the free exercise thereof, are prohibited, yet these sins abound in this town, therefore it is ordained that those guilty therof shall pay for swearing, drinking and Sabbath breaking twelve shillings; for mocking the worship of God, forty shillings.

Recruits for Navy. The Privy Council ordered the Magistrates to beat up for recruits for the Navy here and at Aberdour, each man to have two pounds sterling of bounty, and sixpence a day till he was taken away. On this occasion six men were obtained from Burntisland, and one from Aberdour. At the same time a list of seamen and fishermen was ordered in both towns, that men might be taken by lot if required.

1690. Instructions to Commissioners to Parliament. "The Council, considering that the Protestant religion and the security of the government are in danger from the proceedings of factions and self-seeking men, instruct their commissioner to the parliament, Alexander Ged (in whom they did not seem to have confidence) to vote for the settlement of the church on the ground of the parity of the clergy, as in the times of the purest reformation, and not to delay this on the ground that grievances ought first to be redressed; to vote a supply of money to their Majesties to enable them to raise men for the public security; and if any other subject of debate arise in parliament, the commissioner is ordered to inform the council of it that he may receive their instructions thereanent."

Quartering. The oppressive and tyrannical custom of quartering soldiers on the inhabitants to compel them to pay the government taxes was continued under the Revolution government in the same way as under that of the Steuarts. The Council applied to the Lord High Commissioner for relief on account of the poverty of the town and because of the debt due to it by government for the expense of transporting soldiers from the north. Relief was at first refused, but afterwards some alleviation was obtained by the influence of Lord Raith, but secretly, "as such a favour had not been granted to any Burgh".

Assembly. Octr 16. The Council refused to send a Commissioner to the "General Assembly in respect that no laic can sit there except he be a ruling elder".

Danish Ships. At this time four Danish ships with soldiers on board landed at Burntisland.

Ejection of Minister and subsequent restoration. The Minister of the Parish Mr George Johnstone, being of Episcopal ordination, the Council requested the Presbytery to enquire into his doctrine, which being complied with, he was ejected. In 1691 the inhabitants addressed the Town Council setting forth "that for too long a space they have wanted the preaching of the gospel, whereby they expect the salvation of their souls, and the great increase of crime among them from the want of public worship, and the need they have for the Scriptures being inculcated in their ears"; and prayers that the Bailies and Council, "their patrons", should desire the concurrence of the landward heritors and kirk session in calling a godly minister. The Council met with the heritors accordingly; but on the 25th September Mr George Johnstone was restored to his office by virtue of a letter from the King as it is said. The keys of the church were delivered to him, not without opposition, it being stated that this was done by a plurality of votes. It would appear that in the interval there was a regular service in the church, a voluntary contribution being made for the support of the poor to supply the want of church collections.

Aberdour. The exclusive right to trade in staple wares was now restored to the Burgesses of the Royal

Burghs, and the magistrates were ordered to communicate this to Robertson of Newbigging and Beatson of Kilrie, the Bailies of Easter and Wester Aberdour respectively, and to confer with them as to the terms on which these towns were to be allowed to trade.

1692. Town bankrupt. A process having been raised by its creditors for payment of the debts of the Burgh, some of the Bailies were imprisoned, and the town became bankrupt. It was proposed to assign the whole revenue to the creditors, but the town's Advocate, Mr Monnypenny, advised that some other arrangement should be made. An arrangement was effected accordingly, but in what way, is not recorded. The Bailies, however, were liberated, and the business of the town went on as usual.

Affair of the Bass. One of the Bailies, at the election this year, protested that no person imprisoned or under prosecution about "the affair of the Bass" should be allowed to vote or be voted for. "The affair of the Bass" is several times alluded to but not distinctly specified. Was it those who had been concerned in the imprisoning of the covenanters there during the late reign?

Sea Mills. The long pending question as to the right of the proprietor of the Sea Mills to exact thirlage from the inhabitants of the Burgh was now decided in his favour.

Recruits. There were recruits for the army and navy lodged in the town-house, with a guard of soldiers to attend them. Representations were made to the Privy Council for their removal, but no relief was obtained.

1693. Jas Inglis, Minister, deposed. July 24. Mr James Inglis from St Martins', had been presented to be minister of the parish; but by whom is not said. The Council opposed his admission before the Presbytery of Dunfermline, on what grounds is not stated. The objections of the Council were repelled by the Presbytery, and, with the concurrence of the landward heritors, the case was carried to the superior court. In disregard of these proceedings, Mr Inglis was admitted on the 14th August; but the Council refused to acknowledge him as minister, and took possession of the boxes used for collecting money for the poor, and of the kirk session records.

In 1699, by desire of the council and the landward heritors, the Presbytery held a visitation of the parish, which resulted in Mr Inglis being formally accused of preaching erroneous doctrine, and of negligence in the discharge of his duty. After a long trial, he was suspended from the functions of the ministry sine die, and the parish declared vacant. This Mr Inglis had at first received episcopal ordination, or, as it was expressed, had been ordained by the curates. He dispensed the communion only once during his incumbency.

Military levy. All men belonging to the town, between 16 and 60, fit for military service, were divided into six companies of thirty men each and each company was ordered to provide one man to be sent on service. These six were laid hold of and put in the tollbooth, and sixteen others were ordered to appear fully armed and convey them fully armed to Colonel Mackay's regiment at Cupar. Five were rejected as unfit, and five others were seized and imprisoned to replace them. These being all sent to Stirling, to which Mackay's regiment had gone, were all passed but one, on which the Bailie who accompanied the party gave Major Arnot two guineas, whereupon the man was found fit for service. There were 238 men raised in this way in Fife and Kinross.

Watson's Mortification. Sep. 17. the Bailies informed the Council that they had received a deed of Mortification from John Watson of Dunnikier, executed by the late John Watson, his predecessor, whereby his house and garden in the Midgate were assigned to the Magistrates and Council for the use of three widows of the names of Watson, Boswell and Orrock respectively, or of the widows of men of these names. (These were his own surname, the surname of his wife and that of his mother.) Whom failing, to any other widows the patrons may name. The house and garden were ordered to be divided into three parts, and one part to be assigned to each widow. The Town Council and the proprietor of Dunnikier were nominated joint patrons, and were authorised to present alternately. For the maintenance of these widows, the said John Watson bought from Alexander Aytoun of Inchdairnie part of the lands of Nethergrange. Three fourths of the rents of these lands after deducting public burdens were to be divided equally among these widows; and the other fourth to the Magistrates and Council to be bestowed by them as patrons of the Grammar School, to the master for his teaching as many children of parents residing within the Burgh, who are not able to pay for their children's learning, as the same will extend to at four pounds Scots each child yearly, and though there should not be presented so many children as will extend to the free rent, the said Schoolmaster shall be entitled to the fourth part notwithstanding. For managers of the lands, the Magistrates and Council were nominated as one juncto, and the minister of Burntisland, the heritors of Orrock, Newbigging, Castle and Sea Mills, Inchdairnie, John Durie of Grange, Gedsmill and Binend another juncto. The heritor of Dunnikier was entitled to call the Council and the heritors to account for the management of the Mortification, so far as they interfered therewith. There was at the same time assigned to the minister and elders of the parish and to the Town Council a bond for one thousand merks granted by Sir James Melville of Hallhill to the said John Watson the annual rent of which being forty pounds scots, was to be by them expended in keeping the house in repair and the walls of the garden, after which the remainder was to be expended in equal parts in support of the poor, and in repairing the harbour. But John Watson declared that this bond had been uplifted by his predecessor so that the managers had no claim on him in regard to it. The deed relating to the lands is dated 24th Decr 1684; that to the house 5th May 1689. On 3rd December 1694, three widows were put in possession of the house and garden.

John Watson, the founder of this charity, was employed in obtaining recruits for the military service of Denmark and Sweden, and in the trade of exporting horses to these countries and other parts of the north of Europe. He is referred to as Captain Watson, and was a Councillor and Magistrate. This hospital has afforded a comfortable asylum for a succession of poor widows. The provision for teaching poor children has been made available for that purpose. I believe the number is seldom full. The rent of the land at present (1863) is the value of 32 bolls of barley and 8 bolls of oatmeal at the highest Midlothian fair prices and £5 in money. The expense of maintaining the house is borne by the widows.

1695. Profanity etc. Nov 25. The Council issued an order to the following effect: "considering that the profanation of the Lords-day, profane swearing, absence from public worship and other immoralities are prohibited by several Acts of Parliament from the 3rd of James 6th to the 1st of Charles 2nd, which Acts also forbid the keeping of markets or prosecuting any kind of trade on that day, under the penalty of ten pounds Scots, and ordains that persons frequenting ale houses on Sabbath, except for travel or refreshment, shall pay for the first fault three pounds or be put six hours in the gongs, increasing the penalty for repeated faults till they are to be put in jail, there to remain till they find security for their better behaviour. For excessive drinking and profane swearing" fines were ordered from twenty shillings to twenty pounds according to the station of the offender. In the case of a minister the fifth part of his stipend was to be exacted "notwithstanding all which, and the most holy and just law of God, the foundation thereof, yet it is most manifest that these transgressions abound, to the dishonour of God and the disgrace of the Protestant religion; therefore the Bailies and Council declare that they will see the Acts referred to put in force within this citie", and for their better observance they strictly prohibit all persons within this Burgh to labour on the Lord's-day, or to be found in the streets or to go in Companies or 'vage' to the Shore or Castle Brae, West Shore or fields on that day or any time therof, or to go to ale houses or taverns". They further ordained that no person should bring more than a pint of water from the wells on Sabbath. Parents and masters were to be held answerable for their children and servants; and those who were unable to pay the fines were to be punished in their bodies according to the "merit of the fault".³⁸

Funerals. The Council prohibited all persons from going to the houses of deceased persons, though invited, to eat, drink or smoke tobacco before the funeral.

Thieves etc. Those harbouring "vagabonds, thieves, strangers or those suspected of scandal", were ordered to pay a fine of forty shillings.

Harbour Repairs. Four hundred merks were this year granted by the Convention to be laid out in repairing the West Head, and the town of Inverkeithing was appointed to superintend the work. Was it suspected that former grants had been misapplied?

1698. Military Levy. The Commissioners of supply for the country ordered two men to be sent by the town to serve as soldiers. On this occasion they were balloted for by dice at the sight of Wemyss of Cuttlehill and Leslie of Quarter. None of those liable to the ballot appeared, and those on whom the lot fell having absconded, warrants were issued to apprehend them. The balloted men were to receive forty eight pounds each, and all those liable to the ballot were to pay ten shillings each to make up their sum.

1700. Minister. The care of the parish having become vacant, and the Council finding it an expensive affair to get ministers to preach on Sabbaths, resolved with the concurrence of the landward heritors, to call a "grave and pious man to be permanent minister". This was not easily accomplished. Several were applied to but refused, amongst others Mr Thomas Haliburton, afterwards Professor of Divinity at St Andrews. The government allowance of 500 merks being withdrawn, the remaining stipend was small. At length Mr Thomas Cleghorn was called and appointed in November.

Disfranchisement. Owing to the embarrassed state of the town's financial affairs, the requisite number of Councillors could not this year be obtained, and the Burgh was in consequence disfranchised. The collective community managed the revenue with the concurrence of the creditors. The Council was afterwards restored by a poll vote of the burgesses.

School. The Burgh School was declared vacant by the Council, because they had not funds to pay the stipends of the Master and Doctor; on which both offered to serve without stipend till Martinmas.

Ale. A petition was sent to Parliament for a grant of two pennies on the pint of ale used in the Burgh, setting forth that owing to the decay of trade and the loss of shipping during the late war, they were unable to bear the ordinary expenses of the town, or to maintain the works of the harbour.

Parliament. The Earl of Leven enjoined Bailie Ged, Commissioner to Parliament, to behave himself better at the ensuing session than he did at the last; and said, now since Darien was gone, he expected him to

---

³⁸ The punctuation in this paragraph is incorrect, but is reproduced as it appears in the original.

vote with the court party. Bailie Ged answered that he had voted in the last session as he had been instructed by the Town Council, but that otherwise there was no obligation on him to go with the court party, for they had promised the town the three and a half years' vacant stipend in 1690, but they had got only half a year's stipend; that the government owed money to the Burgh for transporting and maintaining soldiers; and that they had been promised a grant of two pennies on the pint of ale, but had not obtained it. On this a conference was held with the Earl, who promised that all their grievances should be redressed.

Nov. 7. The council instructed Bailie Ged to vote in Parliament.

1st. For securing the Protestant religion as established by law;

2nd. That the settlement of Darien was a rightful and lawful establishment, and to consent to the granting of a supply for carrying it on;

3rd. For a reduction of forces and for a supply suitable thereto;

4th. For rectifying grievances; and

5th. For making such laws as shall conduce to the welfare of the king and kingdom.

Captives. £36 were collected for the relief of some men belonging to Dysart held captives in Algiers.

Revenue. The revenue of the Burgh in 1623, which is the earliest date at which I have seen an account of it, was 484 pounds Scots, equal to £40"4/- sterling, exclusive of the rent of the common lands which was usually about £20 sterling (380 merks Scots), in whole about £60 sterling. The following are the items of which it was composed:-

Anchorage	200 pounds	
Import on Ale	50	"
Small Customs	50	"
Boat Silver	41	"
Duty on Hired Horses	143	"
	484	

These continued with very inconsiderable variation for fully 150 years. At the time referred to, the Minister's and Schoolmaster's stipends were raised by an assessment on the inhabitants, and so continued for upwards of 50 years; but afterwards they were paid from the common revenue of the Burgh.

Discipline. When the Kirk Session was complete, the number of Elders was twenty four (Revelation IV v. 4). The Magistrates of the Burgh were accustomed to attend the meetings for the distribution of money collected for the poor, and on some other occasions. During the whole of the seventeenth century whether prelacy or presbyterianism was in the ascendant, strict discipline was exercised by the Session over the inhabitants of the parish. Those convicted of scolding, flyting, profane swearing and minor offences against good morals were called before the Session and rebuked there or before the congregation. In aggravated cases they were required to ask pardon of those they had offended or injured sometimes on their knees in presence of the congregation. Those convicted of having illegitimate children or of other grave offences were ordained to sit a certain number of Sabbaths on an elevated seat at the south east pillar of the church, in some cases in a white sheet. The number of Sabbaths during which the penitents appeared in this dress were more or less, according to the degree of the offence, but sometimes extended to twenty six. The Romish confessional could show nothing more disgusting, as I imagine, than the examination of the accused persons on such occasions, as detailed in the Kirk Session records.

Searchers. There was a certain number of persons who had a seat appropriated to them in the church, called "searchers". These informed against persons suspected of improper conduct, especially those guilty of profane swearing, drinking to excess, promiscuous dancing, but more particularly Sabbath breaking. Now, one is accused of "vaging" in the fields, at the shore or at the Castle Bank on Sabbath; another is found toasting bread at the fire, or bringing in water on that day; and again one is accused of absenting himself from public worship. For these and similar offences the perpetrators were ordered to appear before the Session to repent and be rebuked. Those who failed to obey were held to be contumacious, and were turned over to the civil power to be imprisoned or banished. The letting of horses or freighting of ferry-boats on Sabbath without leave from the magistrates was forbidden on pain of forfeiting the hire or freight, which was given to the poor. Occasionally a fine was exacted, by way of indulgence I presume, for leave to commit the offence of hiring horses or freighting boats on Sunday. Persons coming to reside in the own were required to bring certificates of character from the minister of the place they had left. Uncertificated persons were refused liberty to reside in the town. About the year 1670 on its being found that the Magistrates were not sufficiently compliant in such cases, and that their authority extended only to banishment from the town, application was made to the Sheriff for the appointment of a Bailie Depute or Kirk Bailie, as he was called, to have power to banish contumacious offenders from the whole parish. The application was granted, but I have seen no notice of its having been renewed.

The Kirk Session. The Kirk Session did not limit their enquiries to open offenders, but instituted investigations into the private affairs of all persons whom they suspected of doing what they considered wrong.

Public Worship. Religious ordinances abounded on Sunday. At the ringing of the nine hours bell, the reader who, during the early part of the century, was usually also schoolmaster, read the prayers and scripture lessons; but after the prayers were forbidden by the Assembly, they were omitted, and the time was occupied in scripture reading and the singing of psalms. This continued till ten o'clock, when the minister came to conduct the regular service. The nine hours bell is continued, but the rest are discontinued. After prayers, a lecture and a sermon with psalms were delivered by the minister in the forenoon. The service in the afternoon was the same as at present. Almost every day of the week there were catechisings, for which purpose the parish was divided into districts called quarters over each of which was placed an elder, in some cases with an assistant called a deacon. The inhabitants of each of these districts were ordered to appear in turn in the church to be catechised; and those absent without a sufficient excuse were afterwards rebuked.

Kirk Session. Persons about to be married appeared before the session, declared their intention and asked permission. I have not observed any case in which permission was refused, but from the tenor of the record it seems to be assumed that they had power to do so. The ecclesiastical authorities appeared to claim the right to interfere in almost every transaction of life. The members of the Session were bound to secrecy under pain of expulsion.

Communion. The communion was celebrated at irregular intervals. Once a year was held to be sufficient, but several years often intervened. When it was resolved to celebrate the communion, the Kirk Session consulted about it some months before, and notice of the day was given to the parishioners. All scandalous persons were interdicted from participating in the communion. Those who were to communicate were furnished with tickets or tokens; and none were allowed to enter the church on the communion Sabbath till the holders of these tokens were provided with seats. Each of the doors had an elder at it to prevent the ingress of those who had not tokens. Till towards the close of the century, there was no communion fast-day, nor any service on the Monday following. After that there were two sermons on the Thursday, two on the Saturday, two on the Sunday morning, eight or nine tables served, and a sermon preached after. Two sermons were also delivered on the Monday following. The collections on sacramental occasions amounted to about 100 libs Scots, which were distributed among the poor. The ordinary collections for the poor were made by the elders going round the congregation in the church with collecting boxes. Special collections were made for assisting neighbouring towns when any unusual cause of distress arose; for relief of seamen held in slavery by the Turks; for maintaining the fabric of the church, for which purpose also the sittings in the church not appropriated to individuals were let at two shillings sterling yearly. On extraordinary occasions the elders went from house to house to collect contributions.

New Bell. In 1708 a new and larger bell than had previously been in use was procured for the church at the cost of £383 Scots.

Poor. The number of the poor on the roll was usually about twenty, the greater part of whom were women. They were paid from two to four shillings Scots weekly. A house was rented to lodge the houseless poor.

Bursar. There were ten pounds appropriated annually for the support of a bursar or student.

Communion Cups. On 12th April 1708, two silver communion cups were presented to the kirk-session by Mr James Callender, writer in Edinburgh, for the use of the kirk at Burntisland. These cups are referred to as being in the session box in 1719. Previous to this, cups were borrowed for the communion service sometimes from Aberdour and sometimes from Kirkcaldy. Those now in use were the gift of Mr James Thomson, minister of the parish, who afterwards seceded from the Established Church and became minister of the Secession Congregation of Burntisland.

Appendix B - Glossary

<u>Notes</u>

1. Currencies. The subject of currencies is sufficiently complex to merit an appendix to itself. The currency terms and conventions which have been used in this book will be found in Appendix C.

2. The glossary has been created specifically for this book. The intention is to give the meaning of unfamiliar words and phrases in the book, or of words and phrases used in an unfamiliar way. The range of equivalents contained in the glossary may therefore be of limited value for other purposes.

3. In the 16th and 17th centuries, words were often written down as they sounded, rather than according to spelling rules. Some of the spellings contained both in this book and in the glossary may therefore be rare, or indeed unique.

A

adstricted - bound
ane - a
anent - concerning
apud - at
astrolabe - instrument for measuring the altitudes of the sun or stars
aught - eight
avocation - vocation

B

bailie, baillie - junior magistrate
baird - beard
bairn - child
bandilier - belt for musket and ammunition
bangstar - bully
baxter - baker
beat up for - go about in quest of
bedsman - dependent; pauper; inmate of a hospital or almshouse
betwixt - between
bier - carriage or frame for bearing the dead to the grave
bigget - furnished with buildings; constructed
bloodwit - quarrel resulting in the effusion of blood; action against a person for bloodshed; fine for shedding blood
bluidy - bloody
boat silver - port dues
bondman - serf
boun for - ready to go to

Boundred - boundary road; boundary between Scotland and England at Berwick-upon-Tweed
box - strong wooden chest with locks, used by a guild to store money and documents
boxmaster - keeper of a guild's box
breeks - trousers
breviary - book containing the daily service of the Roman Catholic church
brig - two masted, square rigged vessel
burgess - freeman; full member of a royal burgh, usually a merchant, shipmaster, or craftsman
burgh of barony - corporation under a feudal superior or baron, who sometimes nominated the magistrates
burgh of regality - burgh of barony enfranchised by crown charter, with regal or exclusive criminaljurisdiction within its territory
burgh, royal - corporate body deriving its existence, constitution, and rights from a royal charter, actual or presumed to have existed
burghal - of a burgh
burnt quick - burned alive
burthen - burden

C

camblet - camel hair; wool and goat's hair
catechising - examination of belief by questioning

147

cinerary urn - urn for ashes

cleanger - cleaner

coket - seal of the custom house

collegiate church - church occupied by two or more pastors of equal rank

commendator - person (often a layman) appointed to administer a benefice or church living, e.g. an abbey

common seal - seal used by an organisation to validate documents

Commonwealth - the republican government in England established by Oliver Cromwell in 1649

concuss - coerce

confit - confection

contumacious - opposing lawful authority with contempt

convenit - convened

conventicle - open air service taken by a dissenting minister

convention - assembly of representatives or delegates

cooper - maker of barrels

cordiner - shoemaker

corslet - defensive garment

cot - coat

councillor - member of a council

covenant - an engagement entered into between God and a person or a people

Covenanter - one who signed or adhered to the Scottish National Covenant of 1638

craig - rock; neck

craig-herring - very large herring

crear - small trading vessel

cromar - merchant keeping a stall; chapman; pedlar

cross-staff - surveying instrument consisting of a staff surmounted with a frame carrying two pairs of sights at right angles

cule - coal

Cyclops - fabled one-eyed giant

D

Danzig - Gdansk, Poland

declarator - action in the Court of Session to ascertain and declare the facts of a matter

decreet - court judgment

defile - long narrow pass

dock silver, docksilver, doksilver - port dues

doctor - assistant schoolmaster

doytes - duties

dung - excrement

dustifoot - travelling merchant; pedlar; vagabond

E

earne - sea eagle

easter - eastern

eln - a measure for cloth, approximately 37 inches or 94 cms

episcopacy - government of the church by bishops

episcopal - governed by bishops

episcopalian - belonging to bishops

F

failyie, failzie - default

fathom - try the depth of

fauldit - clenched

feit - feet

fencible - capable of bearing arms

ferrier - ferry boatman

feu - to vest in someone the right to use land in perpetuity in exchange for an annual payment (feu-duty); that right

flesher - butcher

flyte - quarrel

forasmikle - for as much

forfault - find in the wrong; condemn

fortalice - fortress; fortification

forth - fort; fortress

freeman - one who has the rights of a burgess in a burgh

furth - out

G

gaol - jail

glebe - land assigned to a parish minister in addition to his stipend; land attached to a parish church

gong - latrine

gorgit - throat

graif - grave

grite - great

guild - association for mutual aid

guildry - guild of merchants in a burgh

H

halberd - axe-like weapon
halden - held
hammerman - worker in metal who uses a hammer (e.g. blacksmith, goldsmith)
head - jetty or pier at the entrance to a harbour
head court - periodic meetings of the members of a burgh
head piece - helmet
heretofore - before this time; formerly
heritor - landowner in a parish
hinger - loop for a sword
horning, charge of - charge leading to a declaration that a person is a rebel or outlaw
hurdle - rude sledge

I

inde - thence; from there
Inglis - English
intercommune - commune between or together

J

Jacobite - an adherent of King James VII and his descendants
juggs - an iron collar, chained to a post
juncto - cabal

K

Kalends - 1st of the month (Julian calendar)
King's fine - King's objective
kirk - church
kist - chest; large box or trunk; coffin

L

laic - layman
lawen - bill for drink
Lex Rex - 'Law is King': the title of a pamphlet by a Scottish minister, Samuel Rutherford, which refuted the doctrine of the divine right of kings
Lord Modificator - Church of Scotland arbiter

M

maltman, maltsman - malt maker; maltster; dealer in malt
man-o'-war - warship
manse - residence of a minister of religion
Martinmas - 11 November (Scottish quarter day, old date thereof)
mason - one who cuts, prepares and lays stones
masterless - beyond control
meet - fitting
Michaelmas - 29 September
midding - midden
miln - mill
missal - book containing the complete service for mass throughout the year
moderator - president; chairman
mortcloth - cloak for covering a coffin prior to a burial
mortification - bequest to a charity
mortify - dispose of by bequest to a charity
musqueteer - soldier armed with a musket

N

neive - fist
novo damus, novodamus - charter containing a clause in which the superior of a property grants it 'of new' because of a defect in the original title to the property or because either the vassal or superior wanted to get the conditions of the original grant altered
nunce rebus stantibus - while things remain as they are at present

O

overla - cravat
oversman - chief arbiter

P

pasquil - lampoon
pedlar - one who carries goods for sale
pend - vaulted passage; entrance to a vaulted passage
pestiferous - plague-stricken; causing hurt or loss

Pict - member of the race who inhabited eastern Scotland, northof the River Forth, and who united with the Scots in the year 843 to form the Kingdom of Scotland

pilot - one who conducts ships in and out of a harbour

plurality, a - the greater number

Polonian - Polish

port - harbour; town with a harbour; gateway of a walled town or castle

portus gratiae - port of grace

portus salutis - port of safety

precept - written warrant of a magistrate

presbyterian - of church government by kirk session and presbytery

press-gang - body of sailors under an officer, empowered to impress men into the navy

prime gilt - sum of money paid to the master and crew of a ship for the loading and care of a cargo

prime gilt society - title of a guild representing seamen

privateer - private vessel empowered to seize and plunder an enemy's ships; the commander or crew member of such a ship

procurator fiscal - officer who prosecutes in criminal cases in local and inferior courts

Protestant - pertaining to non-Roman Catholic Christians stemming from the Reformation

provost – civic head of a burgh

prymgilt - see **prime gilt**

Q

quartering - billeting

quhais - whose

R

rave - take away by force

rebukit - rebuked

recusant - dissenter

red - waste material; debris

reeve - steward

Reformation - religious revolution of the 16th century, which gave rise to evangelical and Protestant churches

reft - take away by force

remeid - remedy; redress

remonstrance - formal protest

residenter - inhabitant

roads - roadstead; offshore anchorage

rock and spindle - spinning wheel and spindle

Ronsard - Pierre de Ronsard, French poet (1524-85)

rood - quarter of an acre

ruggit - seized

S

Salec - ancient town in what is now Somalia, which was part of the Turkish Ottoman empire in the 17th century

sax - six

scot and lot - tax levied by a burgh on the burgesses

scurvie - coarse

seal of cause - charter of incorporation of a guild, granted by a town council

shambles - abattoir

shawing - inspection

shipmaster - captain of a ship

showemaker - shoemaker

showing - inspection

smith - worker in metals

stallanger - small trader or craftsman who was not a member of a merchant guild or trade incorporation and who paid a fee for the privilege of carrying on his business at fairs or for a limited period in the community

stent roll - list of persons liable to pay a local tax

stipend - salary of a clergyman

strait - cramped; confined

strength - fortification offering strong resistance

substantious - of substance; wealthy

Suriname - formerly Dutch Guiana, northern South America

synod - assembly of diocesan clergy presided over by the bishop of the diocese during the periods of episcopacy in the 17th century

T

teind - tenth part of, e.g., a harvest, payable as a levy to the church

tertio - third

thereanent - concerning that matter

thirlage - the right which the owner of a mill possesses, by contract or law, to compel the tenants of certain districts to bring all their grain to his mill for grinding

through - lane

togidder - together

tolbooth - booth where tolls and dues were paid to the town council; town house

took - beat; tap

toties quoties - as often as necessary; on every occasion

tron - public weighing machine

tutor - guardian

U

unco - unknown; uncouth; greatly

unfreeman - one who does not have the rights of a burgess in a royal burgh

upbraid - abuse verbally

V

vagabond - wandering idle fellow; rascal

vage - wander idly without good reason

vassal - one who holds land from, and renders homage to, a superior

vavasour - vassal or tenant of a baron, and who also has tenants under him

vennel - alley; narrow street

viol - stringed instrument, precursor of the violin

vivers - food

W

waster - western

wastle - type of bread or scone

watch and ward - watch and guard

webster - weaver

wester - western

whanger - knife or dagger, used at meals and as a weapon

whype - whip

windock - window

witch-pricking - insertion of a long pin of wire into the body of a suspected witch to test for pain sensitivity and the presence of blood

wold - fog; open tract of country

wright - carpenter; joiner

wynd - lane; narrow alley in a town

Y

ye - the

y^t, yat - that

Appendix C - Notes on Currencies Used in Scotland

Throughout James Speed's text, there are references to various currencies in use in Scotland. It is hoped that the following notes will make it easier to understand those references.

In Scotland, until the latter half of the 14th century, coins were worth the actual value of the silver which they contained and the currencies of Scotland and England were broadly equivalent. In 1367, King David II reduced the weight of the silver penny and halfpenny, although both continued to be pure silver. In 1674, an English proclamation decreed an end to the parity of the pennies - in England, a Scots penny would thereafter be worth only three quarters of an English penny. Then, in 1393, an Act of the Scottish Parliament stipulated that the silver content of Scots pennies and halfpennies should be reduced to two-thirds, with the balance made up of base metal. This was the start of what is termed the debasement of the coinage.

These developments were caused by the inability of the Scottish mint to obtain silver in sufficiently large quantities. They signalled the beginning of the divergence of the values of the Scots and English currencies, and this process continued until the end of the 16th century. By 1600, the Scots pound was equivalent to one-twelfth of the English pound. This ratio was maintained until the Union of Parliaments in 1707, when the separate Scots currency was officially abolished (although it continued to circulate for some time after that).

Scots Currency in the 17th Century

For the whole of the 17th century, the value of Scots currency units remained stable at one twelfth of the English units. The following table lists the common Scottish units of currency and their value in English currency.

Scots currency unit	Equivalent in English currency
Penny	One-twelfth of an English penny
Bawbee (= six pence)	One halfpenny
Shilling (= twelve pence)	One English penny
Merk (= thirteen shillings and four pence, i.e. two-thirds of a pound)	Thirteen English pence (approximately)
Pound (pund, lib) (= twenty shillings)	One-twelfth of an English pound (or one shilling and eight pence)

The Scots coins were the halfpenny, the penny, the twopence, the bawbee, the shilling, and the twelve shilling piece. The Scots currency units of merk and pound was solely accounting units, and there were no corresponding coins.

Scottish coins were often in short supply. Forgery was widespread, as was the illegal importation of Dutch and French copper coins. However, these currencies - and English as well - circulated freely in Scotland. James Speed says that, in 1635, "The usual mode of counting money at this time was by dollars, rix-dollars and stivers." This was a reference to the popular Dutch currency.

Some Scots groats (equal to eight pence) and half groats (four pence) were minted in the late 16th century, but Speed's single reference to a groat in the year 1655 was probably to the English version, which was worth four English pence. Speed also used the terms 'angel', which was an English gold coin; and 'white money', which meant silver coins.

The notation used by Speed for a composite sum was, for example, £33"6"8, which means thirty-three pounds, six shillings and eight pence. The abbreviations 's' for shilling and 'd' for pence were also used. Speed sometimes used or quoted the word 'lib(s)' (from the Latin libra, a pound) to denote pound(s).

The purchasing power of a given sum of money was of course much greater in years gone by than it is today. In 1650, with one English pound (or twelve pounds Scots) you could buy goods which today would cost you about £75. Even as late as 1900, your British pound would still get you about £65 worth of goods at today's prices.

The basic currency structure of pounds, shillings and pence lasted remarkably well, right up until 1971 when the United Kingdom changed to the decimal form which we now use. The shilling fell by the wayside, and the penny was redefined to give 100 'new pence' to the pound.

Bibliography and Internet Resources

Burntisland

History of Burntisland: Scottish Burgh Life More Particularly in the Time of the Stuarts (2nd edition) - Andrew Young - Fifeshire Advertiser - 1924

This was at the time the definitive history of the town. The coverage is comprehensive, and the Parish Church receives special attention.

Glimpses of Modern Burntisland: A Series of Impressions and Reminiscences - (Ex-Bailie) William Erskine - Strachan and Livingston - 1930

Based on a series of articles in the Fife Free Press and anecdotal in style, this is an immensely readable history of the town from about 1845 to 1925 - although at times imprecise, and occasionally inaccurate. The book is packed with sympathetic pen portraits of local worthies.

Burntisland: Early History and People - John J. Blyth - Fifeshire Advertiser - 1948

The history of the town from the early days to about 1715. Carefully researched and drawing from a wide variety of original sources. A lot of detail in its 198 pages. Strongly recommended for the serious student of the period.

(Ex-Provost) Robert M. Livingstone, J.P., F.S.A. (Scot.)

Robert Livingstone carried out a great deal of research into the history of Burntisland. He also wrote many articles on the town's history for the Fife Free Press from the 1950s up to his death in 1982. Sadly, his work was never brought together in a single publication, but Burntisland Heritage Trust holds copies of many of the articles, and back numbers of the Fife Free Press are held on microfilm in Kirkcaldy Central Library. His work was recognised when he was elected a Fellow of the Society of Antiquaries of Scotland.

Burntisland: Fife's Railway Port - Peter Marshall - Oakwood Press - 2001

Running to nearly 200 pages and containing more than 140 illustrations, it relates Burntisland's history as a major railway centre, as a ferry terminal and as a port - from the first arrival of the railway to the present day.

A King's Treasure Lost - Howard J. Murray - Silverscreen Print - 1999

The events of 1633, when King Charles I's ferry, the 'Blessing', sank off Burntisland.

Rossend Castle: A Recent Story of Reconstruction after 25 Years of Struggle - L.A. Rolland and Partners - 1977

The fight to save the castle from the bulldozers.

Personal Recollections, from Early Life to Old Age, of Mary Somerville, with Selections from her Correspondence - Martha Somerville - Roberts Brothers - 1876

The Statistical Account of Scotland - edited and published by Sir John Sinclair - 1791-99

Contains a description of Burntisland in the late 18th century.

The New Statistical Account of Scotland - William Blackwood & Sons - 1845

Includes a description of Burntisland in 1836.

Report of the Royal Commission on Municipal Corporations in Scotland - His Majesty's Stationery Office - 1835

Has a fairly detailed, but selective, description of Burntisland in the early 1830s.

Burntisland Online - www.burntisland.net

Contains a large selection of material on the history of Burntisland, and links to other local sites.

Burntisland Heritage Trust: Charles wRex Project - www.kingcharles-wrex.co.uk
Describes the search for King Charles I's ferry, the 'Blessing' of Burntisland, which sank in 1633.

General

A History of the Scottish People: 1560-1830 - T.C. Smout - William Collins Sons & Co - 1969

A History of Scotland (2nd edition) - J.D. Mackie; revised and edited by Bruce Lenman and Geoffrey Parker - Penguin Books - 1978

The Scottish Nation - T.M. Devine - Viking Penguin - 1999

Independence and Nationhood: Scotland 1306-1469 - Alexander Grant - Edinburgh University Press - 1991

Kingship and Unity - G.W.S. Barrow - Edward Arnold - 1981

Burgess, Merchant and Priest: Burgh Life in the Scottish Medieval Town - Derek Hall - Birlinn - 2002

The Early Modern Town in Scotland - edited by Michael Lynch - Croom Helm - 1987

Perth: A Short History - Marion L. Stavert - Perth & Kinross District Libraries - 1981

Scottish Burgh and County Heraldry - R.M. Urquhart - Heraldry Today - 1973

The Town Council Seals of Scotland: Historical, Legendary and Heraldic - Alexander Porteous - W. & A.K. Johnston - 1906

The Scottish Coronation Journey of King Charles I - Robert & Lindsay Brydon - Sporting Partnership - 1993

The Witches of Fife: Witch-hunting in a Scottish Shire - Stuart Macdonald - Tuckwell Press - 2002

Scottish Coins: A History of Small Change in Scotland - Nicholas Holmes - NMS Publishing - 1998

The Royal Commission on the Ancient and Historical Monuments of Scotland: Online Databases - www.rcahms.gov.uk

Dictionary of the Scots Language - www.dsl.ac.uk/dsl

The Survey of Scottish Witchcraft - www.arts.ed.ac.uk/witches

Index

1. Where a page number is in italics, that indicates an illustration.

2. Appendix A is not included in the scope of this index. However, a searchable version of that appendix will appear on www.burntisland.net in due course.